"EGOISM VERSUS EGOISM.—How many are there who still come to the conclusion: "Life would be intolerable were there no God!" Or, as is said in idealistic circles: "Life would be intolerable if its ethical signification were lacking." Hence there must be a God—or an ethical signification of existence! In reality the case stands thus: He who is accustomed to conceptions of this sort does not desire a life without them, hence these conceptions are necessary for him and his preservation—but what a presumption it is to assert that everything necessary for my preservation must exist in reality! As if my preservation were really necessary! What if others held the contrary opinion? if they did not care to live under the conditions of these two articles of faith, and did not regard life as worth living if they were realised!—And that is the present position of affairs." - Friedrich Nietzsche, From *The Dawn of the Day*, Aphorism 90. Translated by J. M. Kennedy.

Table of Contents

Preface

Instead of the usual copied and pasted thanks given to people you've never heard of, I would like to give my sincerest thanks to you. Dear reader, thank you for taking the time to read this book. Believe it or not, it means a lot to an author when even just a single individual takes a genuine interest in their work. Thank you so much.

Who This Book Is Primarily For

I attempted to design this book for those who are open to questioning their religious faith, religious or atheistic debaters who may want a greater breadth of material to critique religious or atheist arguments respectively, for agnostics and atheists who are interested in the possible psychological and social reasons for religious faith, for those who want to challenge proselytizers of the Abrahamic religious faiths with criticisms, and for devout religious people who want to understand why atheists exist and what psychological and moral arguments compel atheists to leave religion. I've found that too many atheist books focus heavily on science as the reason why they leave religion and not enough on the fallacious reasoning of various religions. The primary purpose of this book is to question religious assumptions about the world and to consider why skeptical inquiry would be far more valuable in your everyday life. That is, this book isn't just about why the atheist perspective views religion as false, but also adds the anti-theist perspective of why religion is actively harmful. Not all atheists are against religion, but this book attempts to argue why they should be and why theists should give up on their theism. It would be better to form a new purpose for your life without superstitious beliefs. This book focuses on the major religious faiths of the world; the Abrahamic faiths of Judaism, Christianity, and Islam and the Dharmic faiths of Buddhism and Hinduism.

Why I Wrote This Book

Please note this section is specifically to preemptively answer possible questions pertaining to my inspirations and journey in deciding to write this book. I doubt it'll satisfy all inquiries, but I would hope that it answers most questions about why I wrote this book.

For many years during my youth, I spent a hefty amount of time being a total nerd and listening in fascination to New Atheist debates by Sam Harris and Christopher Hitchens on Youtube. In fact, throughout my time in my senior year of high school and up till early college, I would watch lengthy hours worth of debates by them in my spare time. I would occasionally watch Richard Dawkins too, but he seemed more prone to be annoyed than the other two and he wasn't as well-versed on why the pertinent portions of theology so resolutely defended by theists were either false or illogical. During my undergraduate and graduate years, I became more acquainted with the works of Friedrich Nietzsche because of a video game that used the themes from his philosophical fantasy novel, *Thus Spake Zarathustra*. I eagerly began to read all of his main books and was surprised that much of the vitriol against him seemed either misconstrued or pretentious. Far too many times, people criticized Nietzsche for statements that he never even said. This puzzled me until I learned of what his Nazi-loving sister did to his collection of works, even writing the forgery known as *The Will To Power* through a collection of his notes that people still falsely attribute to Friedrich Nietzsche to this day. It gets more muddled since she and a friend of Nietzsche's added Nazi lingo to the notes of a book that Nietzsche himself had been planning to write. To further add to the confusion, *The Will To Power* was the same title that Nietzsche had in mind. Nevertheless, critics of Nietzsche never actually criticized his works nor displayed any confusion about *The Will To Power*, but rather attributed everything about the man's life to an incident in which he stopped another man from beating a horse before having a mental breakdown due to what is now suspected to be a brain tumor and not syphilis. I found it peculiar that there was this thoroughgoing contempt for decades by Christian theologians and everyday Christians towards Nietzsche for his mental breakdown. There wasn't contempt for his ideas, but rather ridicule for his death far more often than not. Otherwise, many Christians seemed to argue on social media that he had better have repented, which shows their own woeful misunderstanding to the point they had obviously never bothered reading even one of his books before judging him.

I began to notice the same behavior being done to the New Atheist Movement by Christian apologists, Atheists who were religious apologists, and both political sides seem to regurgitate a stream of polemics against them like clockwork instead of criticizing their arguments. For those who don't know, New Atheism was a term coined by the religious apologist Gary Wolf and utilized by the mainstream Western media to generalize Christopher Hitchens, Richard Dawkins, Sam Harris, and Daniel Dennett as extremist atheists. The four self-stylized themselves as the Four Horsemen as a joke when making a lengthy video in which the four discussed topics related to atheism. Similar to Nietzsche, people used ad hominem instead of assessing and criticizing the validity of their arguments. A plethora of opinion pages across many mainstream

Western news organizations, from as early as 2012 to just a few hours ago as of this writing in 2019, began a deluge of articles practically a few months for each year talking in length about how New Atheism was either ignorant, fueled with ire, or had ended. From the sheer breadth of what I read I've learned that New Atheism was over because the New Atheists weren't looking at the bright side of religion like other atheists were. It was too full of aggressiveness and anger to be taken seriously in 2012.[123] It was over in 2013 because those arrogant New Atheists lost their way from

1. [1] Baggini, Julian. "Atheists, Please Read My Heathen Manifesto | Julian Baggini." *The Guardian*, Guardian News and Media, 25 Mar. 2012, www.theguardian.com/commentisfree/2012/mar/25/atheists-please-read-heathen-manifesto.

2. [2] Halla, Barbara. "New Atheism: Missing the Point." *Harvard Political Review New Atheism Missing the Point*, 7 May 2012, harvardpolitics.com/books-arts/new-atheism-missing-the-point/.

3. [3] Murphy, Ian. "Five Atheists Who Ruin It for Everyone Else." *Salon*, Salon.com, 5 Aug. 2012, www.salon.com/2012/08/04/five_most_awful_atheists_salpart/.

defending Liberal principles like that pesky

neoconservative Hitchens who had passed away years

ago[45678], and just to be sure there were a few articles

again in 2014 explaining why New Atheism was over

since they held neoconservative views and young

Liberals were assuredly looking at the bright side of

religion instead of being like those "extremists" who

4. [4] Hobson, Theo. "Richard Dawkins Has Lost: Meet the New New Atheists." *The Spectator*, 12 Apr. 2013, www.spectator.co.uk/2013/04/after-the-new-atheism/.

5. [5] Hussain, Murtaza. "Scientific Racism, Militarism, and the New Atheists." *Israel | Al Jazeera*, Al Jazeera, 2 Apr. 2013, www.aljazeera.com/indepth/opinion/2013/04/201342104 13618256.html.

6. [6] Lean, Nathan. "Dawkins, Harris, Hitchens: New Atheists Flirt with Islamophobia." *Salon*, Salon.com, 29 Mar. 2013, www.salon.com/2013/03/30/dawkins_harris_hitchens_ne w_atheists_flirt_with_islamophobia/.

7. [7] Greenwald, Glenn. "Sam Harris, the New Atheists, and Anti-Muslim Animus | Glenn Greenwald." *The Guardian*, Guardian News and Media, 3 Apr. 2013, www.theguardian.com/commentisfree/2013/apr/03/sam-harris-muslim-animus.

8. [8] West, Ed. "New Atheism Is Dead." *Catholic Herald*, 4 Mar. 2013, catholicherald.co.uk/commentandblogs/2013/03/04/whate ver-happened-to-new-atheism/.

couldn't get along with the religious.[9][10] In 2015, there

was yet another array of news article explaining why

the Four Horsemen were an embarrassment to atheism

and why New Atheism was over because something-

something Islamaphobia and Liberalism.[11][12][13][14] Within

9. [9] Green, Emma. "The Origins of Aggressive Atheism."
    The Atlantic, Atlantic Media Company, 24 Nov. 2014,
    www.theatlantic.com/national/archive/2014/11/the-
    origins-of-aggressive-atheism/383088/.

10. [10] Robertson, Eleanor. "Richard Dawkins, What on Earth
    Happened to You? | Eleanor Robertson." *The Guardian*,
    Guardian News and Media, 30 July 2014,
    www.theguardian.com/commentisfree/2014/jul/30/richard
    -dawkins-what-on-earth-happened-to-you.

11. [11] Sparrow, Jeff. "We Can Save Atheism from the New
    Atheists like Richard Dawkins | Jeff Sparrow." *The
    Guardian*, Guardian News and Media, 29 Nov. 2015,
    www.theguardian.com/commentisfree/2015/nov/30/we-
    can-save-atheism-from-the-new-atheists.

12. [12] Birkenhead, Peter. "Why Do We Let New Atheists and
    Religious Zealots Dominate the Conversation about
    Religion?" *Salon*, Salon.com, 27 Apr. 2015,
    www.salon.com/2015/04/25/why_do_we_let_new_atheist
    s_and_religious_zealots_dominate_the_conversation_abo
    ut_religion/.

13. [13] Bruenig, Elizabeth. "Is the New Atheism Dead?" *The
    New Republic*, 4 Nov. 2015,
    newrepublic.com/article/123349/new-atheism-dead.

14. [14] Gray, John. "What Scares the New Atheists | John
    Gray." *The Guardian*, Guardian News and Media, 3 Mar.

the year 2016, I learned that New Atheists were long
gone and no longer impactful because they were mean
bullies for criticizing religion so harshly but also
Liberalism and Islamaphobia[1516], then in 2017 I learned
that New Atheism was over again with yet another
article about Richard Dawkins behaving poorly on
Twitter or Sam Harris being an Islamaphobe or
Hitchens being wrong to support the 2003 Invasion of
Iraq along with the neoconservative Christians before
his death[17], and then just last year on 2018 I learned

2015, www.theguardian.com/world/2015/mar/03/what-scares-the-new-atheists.

15. [15] Hoelscher, David. "New Atheism, Worse Than You Think." *CounterPunch.org*, 1 Feb. 2016, www.counterpunch.org/2016/01/29/new-atheism-worse-than-you-think/.

16. [16] Gauthier, Brendan. "Never Tweet, Richard Dawkins: Famed Atheist Now Signal-Boosting Nazi Propaganda." *Salon*, Salon.com, 1 Feb. 2016, www.salon.com/2016/02/01/never_tweet_richard_dawkins_famed_atheist_now_signal_boosting_nazi_propaganda/ .

17. [17] Torres, Phil. "How Did 'New Atheism' Slide so Far toward the Alt-Right?" *Salon*, Salon.com, 29 July 2017, www.salon.com/2017/07/29/from-the-enlightenment-to-

how New Atheism was assuredly over again and again in several articles.[181920] Finally, just a few hours ago almost as if ritualistically, the mainstream media assures us that New Atheism is absolutely over because New Atheists are mean people, Dawkins behaves poorly on Twitter, Sam Harris invited Charles Murray and supported his Race Science views on both his podcast and blog, and Hitchens is dead and was wrong about Iraq 2003 because he agreed with

---

the-dark-ages-how-new-atheism-slid-into-the-alt-right/.

18. [18] Cep, Casey. "Why Are Americans Still Uncomfortable with Atheism?" *The New Yorker*, The New Yorker, 24 Apr. 2019, www.newyorker.com/magazine/2018/10/29/why-are-americans-still-uncomfortable-with-atheism.

19. [19] Megoran, Nick, and Russell Foster. "Why the Arguments of the 'New Atheists' Are Often Just as Violent as Religion." *The Conversation*, 19 Sept. 2018, theconversation.com/why-the-arguments-of-the-new-atheists-are-often-just-as-violent-as-religion-95185.

20. [20] Illing, Sean. "Why Science Can't Replace Religion." *Vox*, Vox, 4 Nov. 2018, www.vox.com/2018/10/30/17936564/new-atheism-religion-science-god-john-gray.

neoconservatives.[21] Oh, and upon re-checking when editing this portion of the book, I've found yet another 2019 article about how New Atheism is indisputably over.[22]

Why was this? Why did they continue to argue that New Atheism was in the long and buried past tense every year? Even as far back as 2011, why personal insults instead of criticizing their views on religion by assessing their arguments?[23] Why deter the conversation to their other views instead of just criticizing the arguments they made against religion which is supposedly the main focus of these articles? I

---

21. [21] Poole, Steven. "The Four Horsemen Review - Whatever Happened to 'New Atheism'?" *The Guardian*, Guardian News and Media, 31 Jan. 2019, www.theguardian.com/books/2019/jan/31/four-horsemen-review-what-happened-to-new-atheism-dawkins-hitchens.

22. [22] Hamburger, Jacob. "What Was New Atheism?" *The Point Magazine*, 25 Jan. 2019, thepointmag.com/2019/politics/what-was-new-atheism.

23. [23] Hedges, Chris. "Fundamentalism Kills." *Truthdig*, 26 July 2011, www.truthdig.com/articles/fundamentalism-kills/.

have an assumption that I think is reasonable to explain this bizarre behavior; the data is completely against their argument that New Atheism doesn't continue to have a snowball effect. It is a small one, it may or may not slow down at times, and it is hardly taking hold of the older generations, but for the Millennials and Younger Millennials (Gen Z) across the world, it is only increasing.[24] Not merely agnosticism, but atheism specifically is on the increase and it is especially so within the United States.[25] Different polling data of generational differences in the US show an increase in atheism too.[26] Even worse for religious believers, the

24. [24] Mitchell, Travis. "Young Adults around the World Are Less Religious." *Pew Research Center's Religion & Public Life Project*, Pew Research Center's Religion & Public Life Project, 13 June 2018, www.pewforum.org/2018/06/13/young-adults-around-the-world-are-less-religious-by-several-measures/.

25. [25] "Atheism Doubles Among Generation Z." *Barna Group*, www.barna.com/research/atheism-doubles-among-generation-z/.

26. [26] Cox, Daniel. "Way More Americans May Be Atheists Than We Thought." *FiveThirtyEight*, FiveThirtyEight, 18

last few years have conclusively shown that lack of

belief in a God is correlated with higher IQ and that

atheists are equally as moral as religious believers.[2728]

The only difference seems to be perception; an atheist

and a theist are as likely to do either moral or immoral

actions, but a theist tends to view themselves more

morally than they actually are whilst atheists tend to be

more critical of themselves.[29] That may come as a

genuine surprise to you, but research study after

May 2017, fivethirtyeight.com/features/way-more-americans-may-be-atheists-than-we-thought/.

27. [27] England, Charlotte. "The Reason Why Atheists Are More Intelligent than Religious People, According to Researchers." *The Independent*, Independent Digital News and Media, 2 Jan. 2018, www.independent.co.uk/news/science/atheists-more-intelligent-than-religious-people-faith-instinct-cleverness-a7742766.html.

28. [28] Xygalatas, Dimitris. "Are Religious People More Moral?" *Religion News Service*, 25 Oct. 2017, religionnews.com/2017/10/25/are-religious-people-more-moral/.

29. [29] Xygalatas, Dimitris. "Are Religious People More Moral?" *Religion News Service*, 25 Oct. 2017, religionnews.com/2017/10/25/are-religious-people-more-moral/.

research study has conclusively proven this.[30] For

example, a study of 1,200 children from six different

countries found that children from Muslim and

Christian backgrounds were far less compassionate and

more judgmental than children from secular

backgrounds; the study led credence to the argument

that religion isn't just useless for teaching morality but

may actively harm compassionate moral behavior as

children develop and even worse, religious parents

view their children as more empathetic and sensitive

despite them being less so towards others.[31] One could

argue then, the only difference in morality is that a

religious believer simply brags about themselves more

---

30. [30] "Non-Believers Do Not Lack Morality, Research
Suggests." *ITV News*, www.itv.com/news/2019-05-
27/non-believers-do-not-lack-morality-research-
suggests/?fbclid=IwAR0CmMEZONwS4OqRFotigWhhL
P9i1MUbkGOUvp0RoWVGb4acADr2QGSDlDg

31. [31] Sherwood, Harriet. "Religious Children Are Meaner
than Their Secular Counterparts, Study Finds." *The
Guardian*, Guardian News and Media, 6 Nov. 2015,
www.theguardian.com/world/2015/nov/06/religious-
children-less-altruistic-secular-kids-study.

than atheists while atheists don't tend to brag about themselves on average. One would expect the opposite outcome, but facts are facts. Secular societies have lower murder rates, lower rates of racism, higher happiness rates, and higher rates of gender equality than societies with religious majorities.[32] Similarly within the US, the more religious States have the highest murder rates verses the lowest murder rates in the more Secular States of the US.[33] The hard data is conclusively on the side of secular values and atheism, so why does the contempt for the New Atheist criticism of religion continue to persist?

32. [32] Niose, David. "Misinformation and Facts about Secularism and Religion." *Psychology Today*, Sussex Publishers, www.psychologytoday.com/us/blog/our-humanity-naturally/201103/misinformation-and-facts-about-secularism-and-religion.

33. [33] Niose, David. "Misinformation and Facts about Secularism and Religion." *Psychology Today*, Sussex Publishers, www.psychologytoday.com/us/blog/our-humanity-naturally/201103/misinformation-and-facts-about-secularism-and-religion.

It seemed to me that the mainstream media of the West didn't really value or support critical thinking as they didn't seem to believe that Western Millennials like myself were capable of it. They kept circling back to the same negative talking points about the New Atheists every year as if pretending it was no longer relevant would make it so. They repeatedly emphasized the negatives; acting as if the entire lives and valuable work of these people could be dismissed by a few short paragraphs that emphasized only what was perceived to be negatives about them. The negatives aren't necessarily wrong, but they don't change the positive contributions of these people and they aren't fair to the enormous value that the Four Horsemen of New Atheism brought to the world.

Richard Dawkins has been taking part in Secular conferences speaking on issues of religious violence and intolerance; he's worked along with organizations helping to promote movements like Secular Rescue which seeks to get atheists who are being threatened by death to safety outside of countries like Bangladesh where they're being targeted and murdered by Islamists. Should his assistance in this be outweighed by making crass or stupid comments on social media? Sam Harris collaborated with Muslim Reformist Maajid Nawaz in making a book and a film about issues on reforming Islam; does holding ignorant views on race science outweigh his defense for human rights and his assistance in Maajid Nawaz's quest in reforming Islam? Harris has stated that he's following Nawaz's lead on this approach and he was convinced of it thanks to having a dialogue with Nawaz. Should Hitchens support for a horrible war outweigh and smother his lifelong commitment to the human rights of all people? Should it outweigh his criticism of despots who threatened and harmed the lives of Catholics,

Protestants, Jews, Hindus, Buddhists, and Muslims across the world? Does it matter that he subjected himself to waterboarding in the defense of Muslims who were being waterboarded because he sincerely valued their human rights?[34] Does it outweigh his lifelong criticism of sexism and patriarchy in religious institution and how they harm the lives of the most vulnerable women?[35] His criticism of the Duvalier family and support for the public uprising against the Haitian dictator?[36] Does it discount when Hitchens admitted he was mistaken about Robert Mugabe after he had taken power and Hitchens subsequent support for the popular Catholic human rights protestor, Pius

34. [34] Hitchens, Christopher. "Christopher Hitchens Get Waterboarded | Vanity Fair." *YouTube*, Vanity Fair, 2 July 2008, www.youtube.com/watch?v=4LPubUCJv58.

35. [35] Hitchens, Christopher. "Christopher Hitchens: Hell's Angel: Mother Teresa (English Subtitles)." *YouTube*, BBC News, 7 Jan. 2015, youtu.be/NK7l_IhtKNU.

36. [36] Hitchens, Christopher. "Christopher Hitchens: Hell's Angel: Mother Teresa (English Subtitles)." *YouTube*, BBC News, 7 Jan. 2015, youtu.be/NK7l_IhtKNU.

Ncube, who spoke out against human rights crimes of the Mugabe dictatorship at the risk of his own life?[37] Does it discount Hitchens criticisms of the Catholic Church for taking money and being silent in complicity with those two dictators as they committed human rights crimes?[38][39] Daniel Dennett has written the book *Intuition Pumps and Other Tools for Thinking* in an effort to further promote critical thinking skills among other books. Should he also be marginalized with his negatives being overemphasized repeatedly to mock him like the others have been?

37. [37] Hitchens, Christopher. "The Dark Side Of Religion | Christopher Hitchens @ FreedomFest." *YouTube*, FFreeThinker, 25 Apr. 2009, www.youtube.com/watch?v=iooXQ1-P-0s.

38. [38] Hitchens, Christopher. "The Dark Side Of Religion | Christopher Hitchens @ FreedomFest." *YouTube*, FFreeThinker, 25 Apr. 2009, www.youtube.com/watch?v=iooXQ1-P-0s.

39. [39] Hitchens, Christopher. "Christopher Hitchens: Hell's Angel: Mother Teresa (English Subtitles)." *YouTube*, BBC News, 7 Jan. 2015, youtu.be/NK7l_IhtKNU.

I noticed the identity politics narrative of the mainstream Western media came in full force for several years with assertions such as "Atheists are mostly White males and minorities are mostly religious" as an argument against New Atheists. This narrative was accidentally eviscerated by Ex-Muslim atheists by virtue of the fact that they simply exist and most come from non-European ethnic backgrounds. It was mostly dropped once Ex-Muslim activists became a more prominent force on social media and spoke out against Islam. When the organization, *Ex-Muslims of North America (Ex-MNA)*, began touring colleges for panel discussions about the problems of Islam, pushing for secular values and atheism while occasionally joining in speaking events with New Atheists and needing police security for their own safety while doing so, it became obvious that this narrative of atheism being exclusionary and mostly comprised of white males could no longer be regarded as tenable. The prominence of Ex-Muslims of Pakistani and Middle Eastern descent in Ex-MNA ruthlessly destroyed the supposed racial exclusivity of atheism that the mainstream Western media said was there. The Ex-Muslim women on social media platforms like Youtube and Twitter sharing their stories destroyed the narrative of male exclusivity too. While the focus is mainly in their own countries, Ex-MNA activists and other Ex-Muslim activists in Western societies have helped spread social media blitz campaigns in staunch support of Ex-Muslims within Muslim majority countries fleeing for their lives from persecution. While the mainstream Western media promotes so-called "intersectional feminism" in supposed solidarity with the hijab, Ex-Muslim activists and atheists of other religious backgrounds have responded with videos and criticisms cataloguing the abuses that women who wear the hijab suffer from their own families, how young

women even in the West are killed for not wearing it,

and how it is a symbol of treating women as property of

men under Islamic theology.[40] They've cut through the

Western media's spin in treating Islam as somehow

feminist by pointing out the abuses with a more

authentic intersectional feminist movement that points

out how different religious practices can be abusive and

harmful toward women's rights.[41] However, most

importantly, Ex-Muslims of North America are

building communities for Ex-Muslims who've been

kicked out or attacked by their families for leaving the

religion of Islam. I've personally donated whenever I

can to help them in their goals as they have my full

support at the moment.

---

40. [40] "How World Hijab Day Harms Women." *YouTube*,
Genetically Modified Skeptic, 1 Feb. 2019,
www.youtube.com/watch?v=vVpZ0FZc8SY.

41. [41] "How World Hijab Day Harms Women." *YouTube*,
Genetically Modified Skeptic, 1 Feb. 2019,
www.youtube.com/watch?v=vVpZ0FZc8SY.

To my own chagrin, I wish it hadn't taken me so long to properly recognize the inherent dangers of Islam and it was only the panel discussions by Ex-Muslims of North America that helped me to recognize why Islam was so dangerous. Since then, I've conducted my own research and have become more disgusted with the religion. It reminds me why Free Speech is so vitally important to any democratic society since my perspective has shifted dramatically in these few years thanks to actively searching for research material for this book over the years. Not only did I learn a lot, but I honestly think that this research has helped me grow more knowledgeable as a person. It's an amazing experience to reflect on and it made me truly value the benefits of Free Speech. As an example, I went from staunchly supportive of the journalist Chris Hedges views of New Atheism being too extreme in their remarks on Islam and then I changed my views completely because of my active effort in researching

both the teachings of Islam and the criticisms of Islam

in order to improve my own criticisms of it. I learned of

Ex-Muslims of North America from a random blog post

through a search on the Google search engine, I

watched all of their lengthy college panel videos

throughout 2018, and then used that as a baseline for

delving into understanding how the theology of Islam

functions before forming my own criticisms of it. In

addition, I shared their content on my own blog and

other social media platforms that I used because I think

they're doing valuable work in normalizing dissent for

Ex-Muslims.

This book began as an idea of mine in late 2014

to early 2015 as I delved into reading more psychology

books due to my personal curiosities about human

behavior and the quirks of the human mind. I had

gained this interest from observing religious debacles in

internet forums and watching applied rationality techniques from the organization called Center for Applied Rationality, founded and run by Julia Galef. The information she taught was fascinating to me and on her website she had highly recommended Daniel Kahneman's revolutionary book, *Thinking Fast and Slow.* My personal interest in the book only began after being given the book *Influence: Science and Practice* by Robert Cialdini during my internship by my friendly and intelligent Internship Supervisor and Assistant District Attorney of my local community. After learning the techniques from the book and applying it with surprising results, I decided to purchase Daniel Kahneman's book on a Kindle that my parents generously bought me as a Christmas gift. I initially used it in order to compare current International Relations Theory with human psychology after taking a Political Psychology course for my graduate degree in

Political Science. Around this time, I decided to make a first attempt at a ebook to better understand the ebook process via direct experience so I could correct for any mistakes on self-publishing this book. The ebook in question is called *The Fallacies of New Atheism* and I sincerely regret having written it. I no longer agree with the contents, I wrote it in less than a month, and the only reason I keep it online is to show how my beliefs have radically changed throughout the years through slow and incremental changes in my views. I'd like to believe such a comparison will be able to inspire people by providing solid proof that Free Speech works and that entrenched views can be changed for the better. I'm just sorry it took me so long.

During my journey writing this book, I began realizing that there were too many gaps in my knowledge related to understanding specific issues of different theologies. I had certain issues with

Christianity, especially when communicating with and reading Christian defenses for their faith on online forums. I had believed that the contentions I had considered making must have been thought through and addressed by Christian theologians and that I was being arrogant for making them up until midway through my graduate studies. During my time at a Law and Politics club, which was really just myself and another person talking about daily politics, we sometimes had guests from different clubs or who were curious about the club come over when it piqued their interest. One of the people was part of the Christian club BASIC (Brothers And Sisters in Christ) and invited both of us to join. I considered it because I wanted to know why so many Christians had such a strong degree of confidence in their beliefs and what ultimately motivated those beliefs. I believed there was something I was missing from the picture, since I always found it weird that people of several different faiths could claim to have such confidence in their beliefs but refuse to discuss it. I was under the false assumption that many people had considered criticisms from Hitchens, Dawkins, Dennett, and Harris but had chosen to stick with their religious faith. It didn't occur to me until later that I had used a minority view as a lens and that most people who were familiar with the four had never actually listened to their arguments since most articles about them were just character assassinations that presented them in an extremely negative manner. The leader of BASIC and I agreed that I would just listen in whenever I wanted, I wouldn't have to convert to Christianity or anything of that nature, and I wouldn't have to tell anyone I was an atheist. I could just join and form my own opinions on the matter. I listened to their personal accounts as the club was mainly each individual sharing their personal stories to each other. However, I did begin to notice what I had thought was Friedrich Nietzsche's extremist views against Christianity was instead surprisingly accurate criticisms. The people in the club had really just grown-up in their religion and had been taught to give themselves to Christ when they were little kids without much thought on the matter years later. The leadership of the group held more nuanced views having heard objections to Christianity, but they hadn't been fully introduced to either the criticisms by Western philosophy against Christianity or by the New Atheists. Most seem to study fields in education and STEM from what I had learned. They were very nice people and they didn't really reflect on the truth claims that religion made, it was just part of their upbringing. Some held negative views of those who didn't go to Church regularly and presumed others were either having gratuitous sex or drinking alcohol if they weren't going to Church. I found it bizarre that this was the automatic and implicit assumption whenever they talked of people rejecting their offers to attend a weekly Church gathering. The assumption that others who rejected their offers were committing some specified act that their Church warned about seemed ignorant to me. It was much more likely, given the statistics on the matter, that their peers were probably playing video games, watching sports or anime, browsing social media, and/or doing homework. There was no reason to presume the worst of others, but due to their upbringing pertaining to the teachings of Christianity they did just that. I mostly kept my opinions to myself until the final day, where I debated three club members, including the person who invited me, and we had a very productive discussion on the likelihood of the Christian faith being true as I made comparisons to my knowledge of Hinduism and my explanations for why I had come to the conclusion that there was no evidence for a God's existence. I'd like to emphasize that they were all polite and kind people from my experiences with the club and so were the other club members. However, it became apparent that they hadn't thought as deeply about these issues as I had. Nevertheless, I gained a good baseline to start looking up reasons for Christian truth claims; I began reading the Sermon on the Mount and have formed a critique of it that I've detailed in Part 2 of this book.

Despite all of this, I've been trying to deal with crippling self-doubt over this project throughout the entire process. For six months of the 4 years I should have been working on this book, I doubted myself to the point of not being able to write a single word. I want this book to be the best possible book that I'm capable of making, but I'm struggling with awfulizing the outcome. Awfulizing is essentially forming doomsday possibilities out of one's potential failures to the point it prevents you from acting in your best interests at all.[42] I tried to remind myself that I'm simply a flawed human being and that the work will be done based on the amount of effort I make with middling results. What finally helped was that I made an effort to cut off internet contact when writing. More than any other reason, internet usage destroyed my writing habits and it became increasingly harder to manage that habit when I needed to do research online. I struggled with the fear that the arguments I was making was too arrogant and that ultimately nothing I wrote would be of any value or change any minds. Yet, I held the paradoxical hope that my book could help somehow change the world for the better, but I'm sure almost every author has aspirations that their ideas are truly unique and can influence the wider society.

---

42. [42] Dryden, Windy. *Overcoming Procrastination*. Sheldon, 2000.

I wanted this book to be the sum total of my criticisms of religion and I kept adding new parts because I wished to address almost every issue that I saw come-up in religious debates which didn't have compelling responses. The first part is about general criticisms of religion, the second part is about particular failings in each of the major religions, and the last portion is an attempt to share some of the history of religious violence so people have a clearer historical context on the violence perpetuated by religious norms and values. Of course, it is impossible to criticize every specific denomination of a religion and to highlight all instances of historical abuses, so I tried to thoroughly explain as much as I possibly could. I relied upon outside sources and cited experts for particular topics that were outside of my realm of focus. I hope that this critique is useful and helpful for most readers. The critiques within this book for Part I and Part II are based upon a mix of Nietzschean philosophy, social and cognitive psychology, logical fallacies, and my own personal critiques utilizing those methods. I attempt to give full explanations on how religion and the major religious belief systems harm humanity or don't make much sense to follow when seen through these perspectives.

To conclude this segment, I spent approximately four years researching for and writing this book to criticize religion on the basis of logical fallacies, social and cognitive psychology, and Nietzschean philosophy because I want to contribute however much I can in ending certain harmful religions and reforming other religions to lessen the probability of their harm. I honestly grappled with self-doubt throughout the entirety of those four years regarding this book and kept feeling that whatever clear points I had would either be viewed as ignorant on my part or that this book just wouldn't matter. Despite my desires to write the book, I began to fear that it could lead to violent reprisals for Muslim minorities and Sikh minorities in the West. During my college years, due mainly to reading Chris Hedges articles in more depth, I had gradually changed my views on the New Atheist movement. I began believing them to be well-intentioned but too focused on emphasizing religion over any other factor for the reasons of sectarian violence and felt religious tolerance was perfectly valid as an alternative. I still largely agreed with their views on the vacuous nature of religious faith and I still wanted to share my criticisms of religion, but I feared doing so could unintentionally engender violence against Muslims due to anti-Muslim bigotry and Sikhs who are wrongfully maligned as associated with Islam in the US. For six months of those four years, I nearly abandoned the project entirely and even considered deleting the entire book (by which time, I had a done several draft revisions of Part I and Part II) because I feared that my desire to exercise my Free Speech could be harmful. It was only after listening to Ex-Muslims of North America's panels that I realized I had allowed my desire for religious tolerance to delude me. I had thought sharing my views could be harmful, yet here was a community that had to live with threats to their very lives for speaking out against a religious faith they had left. They spoke out against Islam, because of their compassion for victims of Islam and they argued the primary victims of Islam were Muslims themselves. Despite the security threats to their lives, some of them being forever forced to flee their countries of origin from the Middle East and being effectively ex-communicated by their families, often they were the first voices aiding those who were outright hunted down to be killed in Islamic majority countries for leaving Islam by making their plights known more widely through social media, and they still spoke in defense of the human rights of people - including their own families - some of whom wanted them dead or excommunicated. That is not a hyperbole or a misrepresentation. The danger of Ex-Muslims being killed is especially true when you factor the lives of Ex-Muslims in Islamic majority countries. Ex-Muslims of North America advocates for Secularism and Enlightenment values like Free Speech, Human Rights, and the Separation of Church and State. Primarily, they work to normalize dissent within North America and build communities for Ex-Muslims who have been kicked out of their families. It was thanks to watching their lengthy videos that I regained confidence in continuing this book and recognizing the importance of criticizing harmful beliefs. My sincerest apologies to all erstwhile allies who believe in the concept of *Religious*

Tolerance, but human rights can only be defended by criticizing ideologies. If religious tolerance doesn't defend human rights, then it is worthless and criticizing harmful belief systems should take priority. For a brief period, I had believed religious tolerance could support human rights, but I was forced to recognize that the overwhelming evidence is against me. When Christopher Hitchens said and wrote that religion poisons everything, I believe that he was on the mark far more than most people would like to acknowledge and that the world's changes after his passing only further proved him right. Antitheism may seem extreme or hateful, but I have found the position represents those who are deeply concerned for the human rights of others. And unlike religious tolerance, which shuts down debates and discussions on religiously motivated violence - especially of a particular religion, antitheism defends the human rights of all religious people who

suffer persecution and distinguishes people such as
Muslims from a hateful set of ideas such as Islam. I
don't feel that making this shift in views requires an
apology, if antitheism is extreme then I would argue it
is only extreme in its compassion for the human rights
of others. I don't see such a strong concern for human
rights from those who advocate for religious tolerance,
but only from those who advocate for criticizing
harmful religious beliefs. As such, I changed my views
yet again because my primary concern has always been
for the human rights of others. Criticizing toxic beliefs
is an act of compassion and it is an act of compassion
that the views of religious tolerance finds inconvenient
and doesn't share. I have written this book to add
however much I can to that conversation. I doubt
anyone will, but please believe me when I say that I
wanted so badly to believe that religious tolerance was
possible and that a peaceful world filled with such

parts of Friedrich Nietzsche's philosophy increase exponentially in the immediate aftermath. I felt what I had questioned to be a strange, dismal, and counterintuitive belief in the ancient atheistic branch of Hinduism more affirmed than ever before the crash.

I had previously believed, before this near-death experience, that I would be clinging to a belief in a higher power when faced with such a horrific event because I saw myself as weak and malleable to nonsensical delusions in times of true suffering, but instead no such belief in a higher power or a God ever came about after suffering through a near-death experience. Neither immediately after the crash nor later on at the hospital or even in the weeks and months that followed. It genuinely surprised me in the aftermath of the crash that I felt no compulsion to believe in any such higher power, because I thought for sure that in times of desperation that I would prove to myself that I was weak and needed ignorant delusions to feel safe since I was only human. Yet, it never happened. My strengths in my beliefs; the atheistic variant of Hinduism, my penchant for Nietzschean philosophical beliefs, and my personal dreams were what

I felt strongly attune to in the wake of the near-death experience. It hadn't radically changed my life as pop culture is wont to depict of such events, it just made my prior philosophical and scientifically inclined beliefs stronger.

I became disillusioned by the fact my family's car insurance company, Geico, hadn't done any real work with finding out who was at fault for the accident and because there was no third-party witness, they wouldn't put any value on my side of the story. The police did not either and even incorrectly placed my father's name as the driver, even after I had physically handed them my driver's license. Thus, Geico simply labeled me culpable because it was easier for them than doing any real work in helping me with my situation. They didn't consider my pain and suffering, they just saw me as another nameless and faceless commodity that they needed to clear the paperwork of as quickly as their disorganized business model would allow. Any questions or concerns I had while I was in physical pain was met with mockery and derision by Geico staff on the phone. They immediately demanded that I get off their insurance policy a month after going to physical therapy and questioned why I needed it, even after the doctor

noted the dislocation in my neck and the physical therapists noted the

partial immobility on the knee that had been impacted in the crash.

All of the paperwork documenting these facts had already been sent to

them by the physical therapy clinic that I was going to for treatment.

Due to their lack of doing any real paperwork, they demanded I

resubmit the information to verify and threatened to cut the program

and footing me the bills despite the fact my father had coverage that

insured it was fully paid. Overall, I learned the hard way that saving

car insurance on televised commercials meant a disorganized entity

would mock any horrifying suffering you go through, potentially what

your children could go through, and that they genuinely don't care

whether you live or die so long as they can save costs since that was

their entire business model. I can only speak from my own

experience, but if you want your children mocked upon suffering a

horrifying car crash with life-threatening injuries so they can relive

the trauma, then Geico is definitely for you. They genuinely won't

care what you or your loved ones suffer upon being on the receiving end of an accident regardless of how brutal the injuries are and won't do any work to prove your case because they only value you for your money and don't care about your life. Not that what I say will matter, predatory companies like Geico will always find some way to stay afloat and harm the public while making funny commercials to give them a sense of ease. The ignorance of the US public will always be met with the savage assault by the powerful government institutions and businesses of the United States.

While that may seem emotionally charged, it's important to place blame where it is deserved to avoid following nihilistic patterns of behavior whereby a person blames "reality" or "society" or themselves under the perception they're uniquely stupid and thus too dumb to do anything productive after suffering a tragedy. I did struggle with such notions, but fortunately, a quote from one of Nietzsche's philosophical books helped relieve some of the tension. To paraphrase, the philosophical aphorism simply states an obvious truth in a more insightful manner: that it isn't the world that makes us depressed, angry, or imposes suffering upon us; but rather, the human world that enforces this upon us. The man who sped in a 40 mph roadway at what I suspect to be 70-80 mph before forcing the breaks just before their car collided with my driver door was using a man-made object that nearly killed me and caused lifelong neck pain as a direct result of the impact, but the car I was using opened up side airbags to reduce the physical damage so that my knees, head, and sternum weren't permanently damaged from the impact. Should I thank a specific deity for that, as most religious people in that situation likely would? No, because just as we should place equal responsibility on that which harms us, we should place equal responsibility on those who help us whether from the past or the present. Just as it is man-made inventiveness and laws that harmed me, it is man-made human ingenuity and inventiveness that created the side-impact airbags that softened the impact upon my body and prevented any further injuries beyond my neck suffering from a dislocated hernia and quite possibly precluded my death. I'd like to take a moment to thank the Swedish researchers and engineers who created the side-impact airbags in 1994 for saving my life. Your contribution to consumer safety has my utmost gratitude as I may not have been alive today, if not for your hard work and concern for road safety. Additionally, the Honda car company has my thanks for adding such car safety measures on the car my family purchased, and the physical therapy clinic for giving me treatment. I will happily thank all of those people who made such important decisions with respect to public safety, but thanking a deity is utterly inconsequential to the positives and negatives of what happened to me.

If I were to thank any Goddess or God surviving the accident, should I also thank them for causing the accident? Should I simply praise them for an experience, simply because I had no choice but to go through the experience? Should the reality of my experience necessitate that I praise a deity in gratitude? If a God is responsible for my survival, then surely they're also responsible for causing the situation in the first place? Irrespective of whether a demonic figure exists to direct evil in the world, or even if human sin, bad karma, or freewill exists; surely the origin point of my experience would have to be a deity willingly and knowingly formulating the terrible occurrence beforehand and then causing the event? If it were not so, then certain religious believers would be wrong in claiming that their God is all-knowing, omnipotent, and has a plan. So then, such a deity would be deserving of blame and praise for any experience a human being goes through in equal proportions regardless of how negative or positive the experience is.

Religion is commonly defended by our personal experiences in life. People often use anecdotes to defend their beliefs and usually say that they have faith that their life will improve through belief in God. Being positive is argued as a reason for why a particular religious faith is true and the majority of people use faith as a guidepost for everyday activities. This creates a convoluted and harmful standard that people live under but don't recognize. As a consequence, many people don't give much consideration to religion because they feel it is normal. It is no different than observing the harmful effects of believing in the lucky chance of winning the lottery. People who play the lottery and have faith in the belief of good fortune often don't give any consideration to the detrimental effects of their gambling habit and they don't consider the real mathematical odds of being the winner. They make false assumptions about the likelihood because they're unable to differentiate the relative and absolute values of winning the lottery. For example, let us say there are 60 different possible combinations of numbers on a set of ten numbers in a ticket and the winning combination is 1234560789. What are the odds of winning the lottery by that combination of tickets?

Shocking as this may seem, the winning odds are determined by the number of possible combinations of the ticket. Thus, because there are sixty possible combinations at the start, the actual chances of winning are 60 x 59 x 58 x 57 . . . and so forth. The only winning ticket is 1234560789 so every other combination from 1-60 will lead to a waste of your money. With respect to a real life lottery in the US. your chance of winning the Powerball is around 1 in 292 million for any set of combinations as of 2016.[43] The population of the US is

1. [43] Barker, Jeff. "Statisticians question logic of buying multiple lottery tickets as jackpot rises to $1.5 B." *Baltimoresun.com*, 13 Jan. 2016, www.baltimoresun.com/business/bs-bz-powerball-maryland-odds-20160111-

around 320 million and the population of the largest US State is California which has approximately 38 million residents. Hypothetically, if Powerball operated exclusively in California and all the people in California bought one Powerball ticket, then there would only be a 13 percent chance of any individual Californian getting the winning ticket and an 87 percent chance that nobody in the State would win. If every Californian – from infant to adult – bought seven tickets each then only a single person among them would win the Powerball lottery. A single lottery gambler within the US buying more tickets won't change this fact or strengthen the odds to any significant degree, even in the context of the Powerball being bought throughout the US. This is because even purchasing an absurd number of tickets such as 2000 tickets would only result in a 0.0000069 percent chance of winning. For readers who purchase lottery tickets; please compare the combinations of real life tickets that you know of. Count the possible combinations of each set of numbers or – in some cases – just look at the back of the ticket where it explains the odds of

---

story.html.

winning. Usually, the lottery ticket combinations exceed the amount of people living within the State by a wide margin. Now, consider the odds written on your lottery tickets with the amount of people in your local county. Please keep in mind, the amount of times you play, how old you are, and what special meaning is absolutely inconsequential to the total combinations of numbers that are possible. What matters is the combination of numbers and placing personal attachment to a specific sequence of numbers – like a child's birthday – is utterly meaningless. Lottery players are simply being duped and using irrational thinking to waste their savings on gambling. This means that millions of people both within your country and across the world who strongly have faith that they will win the lottery believe in a falsehood; it means that people who play the lottery out of habit are still squandering their money away on a useless and detrimental pastime. It shows that millions of people can be utterly wrong despite the popularity of a belief throughout an entire country. The defensive arguments that lottery gamblers make, such as the statement "You never know" only demonstrates a basic ignorance of how lotteries function. The gambler is admitting their ignorance by making such a statement. This can be proven on a demonstrable mathematical level, if need be. Lottery gamblers have been duped by their faith in the power of luck and good fortune. Scholars from college professors to business investors have privately regarded the lottery as a stupidity tax.[44]

The duping is largely because gamblers use personal experience – their own anecdotal events in life – and selectively focus upon the lottery winners who won millions. Seeing people online or on television smiling with a giant check reinforces the hope that they can win too. They have not considered the millions of people who have played the lottery throughout their lifetime and never won. This is despite the fact they largely meet and speak with a small percentage of them every day and are likely among that group of people who will never win because of the mathematical probability. Even if small

---

2. [44] O'Brien, Matt. "Why you should never, ever play the lottery." *The Washington Post*, WP Company, 14 May 2015, www.washingtonpost.com/news/wonk/wp/2015/05/14/why-you-should-never-ever-play-the-lottery/?utm_term=.60541de1ad73.

rewards such as $3000 is won by a lottery player, it wouldn't be a gain because they would have to compare the amount of that single small win with the total amount lost during their lottery ticket purchases throughout the years. Their purchasing power was diminished on every ticket that was not a winner and wasted. A community of lottery gamblers makes the self-destructive habit seem normal because of the availability of examples. Seeing people play at nearly every gas station, grocery store, and corner store might convince people that it's not harmful because millions of people do it every day.[45] If you play the lottery, just make a simple list of how much you've spent on the lottery versus how much you've earned from the lottery; keep it honest and don't skim over one or two dollar purchases.

Lottery gambling shows that millions of people can be utterly wrong about the normal activities that they partake in, it shows that despite repeated behavior they don't realize the negative

---

3. [45] Cialdini, Robert B. "Chapter 4: Social Proof (98-140)" *Influence: Science and practice*. 4th ed., 21st Century Bks, 2002.

consequences of wasting money that could be saved for their future, it shows that using a large population size to justify a belief isn't a good reason at all to argue in favor of that belief, it shows that people can have positive beliefs used against them and harm them both emotionally and financially without them recognizing the problem, and that relying on "luck" through arguments from their own lack of knowledge of the odds can cause people to waste years of their life on a harmful belief. All of this is a consequence of using only personal events – anecdotes – and a belief in a metaphysical "luck" as a way to justify ones choices. A community that helps reinforce the normalcy and treats the lottery as a positive activity can only serve to harm the individual. People who understand the mathematics behind the lottery don't fall for the lottery trap; they recognize the personal experiences and faith of the lottery gamblers is a self-reinforcing falsehood. They don't follow the crowd via justifying their actions by the amount of lottery players around them who strongly believe in the fanciful qualities of the lottery. The scope of the population size is recognized as a logical fallacy compared to the statistical probabilities of a specific outcome happening. For comparison, within the US, the lifetime statistical likelihood that I would have died in the car crash that happened to me is approximately 1 in 572, the lifetime odds of dying from an assault by firearm is approximately 1 in 285, the lifetime likelihood of dying from an accidental firearm discharge is approximately 1 in 8527, the likelihood of any random person being hit from a lightning strike on an annual basis is approximately 1 in 17 million, and the annual likelihood of being drowned in a flood is approximately 1 in 12 million.[46] As mentioned prior, the likelihood of getting the winning ticket on the Powerball is 1 in 292 million and for the Mega Millions, it is approximately 1 in 300 million.[47] If you live in the US, then you and I are far more likely to be killed in car crashes, shot dead, killed by fire, drowned, and struck by lightning than we'll ever be of winning the Powerball or the Mega Million lotteries.

4.   [46] "Facts   Statistics: Mortality risk." *Facts   Statistics: Mortality risk | III*, www.iii.org/fact-statistic/facts-statistics-mortality-risk.

5.   [47] Isidore, Chris. "These are your odds of winning Powerball or Mega Millions." *CNNMoney*, Cable News Network, money.cnn.com/2018/01/04/news/powerball-mega-millions-odds/index.html.

Anecdotes

A focal problem with anecdotes is that they can be argued in favor of any position; no matter how contradictory, racist, homophobic, or even positive. Anecdotes are a logical fallacy because they don't account for the actual statistical figures of a given subject and instead argue in favor of a position through personal events or isolated incidents.[48] Some of these anecdotes can be inferred from viewing events on television or online. An example would be the statistics on wars. Despite what is displayed on the news, wars have been on the decline since the 1970s.[49] After World War 2, there has been a huge drop in the ratio of violent conflicts throughout the world[50], but this sounds ridiculous when war stories occur on the news virtually every week. Evidently, the only reason that the

6. [48] Kahneman, Daniel. Chapter 12: The Science of Availability (129-136). *Thinking, fast and slow*. Farrar, Straus and Giroux, 2015.
7. [49] Roser, Max. "Visual History of The Rise of Political Freedom and the Decrease in Violence." *Visual History of The Rise of Political Freedom and the Decrease in Violence*. Web. 3 Jan. 2016.
8. [50] Roser, Max. "Visual History of The Rise of Political Freedom and the Decrease in Violence." *Visual History of The Rise of Political Freedom and the Decrease in Violence*. Web. 3 Jan. 2016.

majority of people perceive that humanity has become more violent is
the easy coverage of violent conflicts as they are happening. During
the era of newspapers, this was not possible. The modern media has
allowed people across the world to gain insight on conflicts far
removed from their location and NGOs have allowed people to give
aid to suffering refugees to a greater extent than in the past. A greater
awareness of these violent events has actually allowed better
responses for the people who are suffering. Yet, the erroneous
perception that humanity is becoming more violent still remains
because of people's repeated exposure to news about different wars
across the world.[51]

Religious anecdotes are just as problematic. If, for example, a
child is suffering from cancer but is cured either through medical
treatment or the cancer disappears because their immune system
successfully fought it off then religious believers often say that God
has cured the child of cancer. If, however, the child regrettably dies of

---

9. [51] Kahneman, Daniel. Chapter 13: Availability, Emotion, and Risk (137-145).
    Thinking, fast and slow. Farrar, Straus and Giroux, 2015.

cancer then religious believers are most likely to – after giving honest condolences – say the child is with God in the afterlife. Thus, what changes aren't the horrible circumstances of the events but rather the interpretation of the events to make the believers feel better about death. It is the same for children in third world countries; the majority of people in first world countries ignore the issue of starving and dying children in third world countries under the basis that it has nothing to do with their personal lives. People often tout that the dead children are in heaven and no longer suffering. However, what changes aren't the horrific circumstances of innocent children dying from the world having failed them, what changes is a religious believer's perception of the event. The change in perception is for the comfort of the religious believer so that they don't have to think deeply or feel horrible from knowing there are children dying from starvation in third world countries. Sadly, this creates another problem, predatory missionary groups use anecdotes to their advantage on unsuspecting and uneducated people to argue in favor of their religion by holding people hostage; examples can vary in severity. There are cases of Christian missionaries pretending a transport vehicle is broken down until impoverished people living in a third world country pray to the religion of the missionary group to get the bus "working" again.[52] Worse still, some Christian missionaries are known to refuse health services until impoverished people convert to Christianity or pay a hefty fee for transport.[53] The level of apathy for the plight of the third world has prompted wealthy families to create public works projects like the Gates Foundation to combat issues related to healthcare which will hopefully stymie Missionary exploitation of the third world.[54]

Anecdotes and Symbolism

10. [52] Goldberg, Philip. "Missionaries in India: Conversion or Coercion?" *The Huffington Post*, TheHuffingtonPost.com, 19 Feb. 2014, www.huffingtonpost.com/philip-goldberg/missionaries-in-india_b_4470448.html

11. [53] Goldberg, Philip. "Missionaries in India: Conversion or Coercion?" *The Huffington Post*, TheHuffingtonPost.com, 19 Feb. 2014, www.huffingtonpost.com/philip-goldberg/missionaries-in-india_b_4470448.html

12. [54] Boseley, Sarah. "How Bill and Melinda Gates helped save 122m lives – and what they want to solve next." *The Guardian*, Guardian News and Media, 14 Feb. 2017, www.theguardian.com/world/2017/feb/14/bill-gates-philanthropy-warren-buffett-vaccines-infant-mortality.

Anecdotes often require symbolism in order to maintain the feelings of normalcy. Religious symbols are often displayed to instill feelings of hope; especially during harrowing times. Religious symbolism is often utilized in books, films, and sometimes in court proceedings to create a veneer of God defending the rights of the people for the sake of equality and to further symbolize moral goodness. Flag symbols in the background of a superhero character, religious symbols such as the cross, and of course the statement "In God We Trust" behind the court judge serve as common examples of these symbols. Symbols help facilitate the pattern recognition bias within humans; that is, perceiving a correlation between two different events where there is none.[55][56][57] When justice is served for the public good, religious believers see a correlation with the success of the legal system and God's will. Instances of justice failing to help people or

---

13. [55] Kahneman, Daniel. Chapter 4: The Associative Machine (50-58). *Thinking, fast and slow*. Farrar, Straus and Giroux, 2015.
14. [56] Kahneman, Daniel. Chapter 6:"Norms, Surprises, and Causes" (71-78). *Thinking, fast and slow*. Farrar, Straus and Giroux, 2015.
15. [57] Kahneman, Daniel. Chapter 7: A Machine for Jumping to Conclusions (79-88). *Thinking, fast and slow*. Farrar, Straus and Giroux, 2015.

unfair laws imposed upon people are often ignored and the public gains a fallacious understanding of what the law is really meant to be. Laws are dependent upon interpretation; juries are to determine if a particular incident broke a set of rules. Yet, when instances such as the failure of the law are displayed then it is argued that humans are imperfect. So what good is the symbolism in the first place? Believing that justice is preordained to God's will is a deception. It is a deception that is used against individuals who believe in it and it willfully ignores instances of failure in the justice system.

An example of this nefarious deception, the faultiness of symbolism, can be shown by the following fact about the law: most US citizens believe that US police officers have a lawful duty to protect them from any harm. This is legally false; a Supreme Court decision in 2005, Castle Rock V. Gonzales, determined that police protection was not a protected entitlement under the 14th amendment and that the protection of private citizens was not part of the public duty doctrine that the police are required to uphold.[58] In the context of the case itself, Gonzales noticed her children missing from her front yard and called the police to inform them that her estranged husband had probably taken them. He wasn't allowed to take them during that day because of the custody rules in place for when he was could spend time with the children. The police didn't take the claim seriously because they had many spousal complaints similar to Gonzales's call; Gonzales tried calling the police at several times during the hours and even went to the police station to show the protective court order whilst desperately asking for help. The police refused to do anything, the police officer at the desk took a lunch break after hearing her pleas, and the next day her ex-husband committed suicide by cop. The officer at the scene found the dead bodies of Gonzales's three young children in the trunk of the ex-

---

16. [58] No. 04-278 TOWN OF CASTLE ROCK, COLORADO v. JESSICA GONZALES.
https://www.justice.gov/sites/default/files/osg/briefs/2004/01/01/2004-0278.mer.ami.pdf 1-45. Supreme Court of the United States. 27 June 2005. *Justice.Gov.* United States, 27 June 2005. Web. 5 Feb. 2018. <https://www.justice.gov/sites/default/files/osg/briefs/2004/01/01/2004-0278.mer.ami.pdf>.

husband's car.[59] The trial went to the Supreme Court and the case was dismissed on the basis that Gonzales's children and by proxy all Americans had no legal right to police protection within the United States. According to the ruling, the police don't have to help you, even in instances when you are being robbed, assaulted, raped, or murdered.[6061] The Castle Rock police department was quick to reframe the event in order to blame the grieving mother and politicians hailed the decision by focusing strictly on how police had to make tough decisions when on the field of duty. What wasn't mentioned was how the US government, from the local to federal level, no longer had to pay any damages to victims who suffered from

17. [59] Greenhouse, Linda. "Justices Rule Police Do Not Have a Constitutional Duty to Protect Someone." *The New York Times*, The New York Times, 28 June 2005, www.nytimes.com/2005/06/28/politics/justices-rule-police-do-not-have-a-constitutional-duty-to-protect.html.

18. [60] No. 04-278 TOWN OF CASTLE ROCK, COLORADO v. JESSICA GONZALES. https://www.justice.gov/sites/default/files/osg/briefs/2004/01/01/2004-0278.mer.ami.pdf 1-45. Supreme Court of the United States. 27 June 2005.*Justice.Gov*. United States, 27 June 2005. Web. 5 Feb. 2018. <https://www.justice.gov/sites/default/files/osg/briefs/2004/01/01/2004-0278.mer.ami.pdf>.

19. [61] "CASTLE ROCK V. GONZALES." *Legal Information Institute*, Cornell University Law School, 21 Mar. 2005, www.law.cornell.edu/supct/html/04-278.ZS.html.

the police failing to uphold their supposed duty in protecting the citizens from harm.[62] The Supreme Court of the United States had determined that the lives of children – who were ages 7, 9, and 10[63] – were less important than the government losing sums of money.

If you are a US citizen, you may have feelings of disbelief upon reading the aforementioned paragraph. After all, you've likely grown up with an entire culture of police dramas like Law and Order, NCIS, and other American TV shows with a plethora of episodes depicting valiant police officers doing their utmost to aid rape victims, children, and the wrongfully accused. These depictions usually consist of a main character having a strong personal connection with the victims to help them cope with the horrible events. The reality of the law seems ridiculous in comparison to what you might believe

20. [62] Teitelbaum, Joel, et al. "Town Of Castle Rock, Colorado V. Gonzales: Implications for Public Health Policy and Practice." *Public Health Reports*, Association of Schools of Public Health, 2006, www.ncbi.nlm.nih.gov/pmc/articles/PMC1525280/.

21. [63] Greenhouse, Linda. "Justices Rule Police Do Not Have a Constitutional Duty to Protect Someone." *The New York Times*, The New York Times, 28 June 2005, www.nytimes.com/2005/06/28/politics/justices-rule-police-do-not-have-a-constitutional-duty-to-protect.html.

about the justice system; what you may not have realized is that you are using aspects of fiction to fill the gaps in your understanding of reality. You may have unintentionally used fiction as a substitute to fill in what you didn't know because we humans feel safe when we have a coherent understanding of the world. These stereotypes have been formed by "mental shortcuts" that you have developed regarding the world around you and your possible ignorance of the real law could be utilized against you. You may have formed a coherent story and expectations based on what you knew about the law but the fact remains that you probably didn't know about the actual laws governing you.

Psychological studies have found that, due to our increasingly complex societies, people use mental shortcuts to quickly determine what different subject matter represent and mean. These mental shortcuts are referred to as judgmental heuristics; snap judgments made out of the availability of the information in our personal lives or through repetitions that we observe on social media.[64] This is natural human behavior because we cannot make deep insights about every single subject matter that we are confronted with even in a single day. As a consequence, stereotypes about certain jobs, organizations, and different types of people abound and will probably always exist. These psychological shortcuts are only worsened by our human bias to see pattern recognition from anecdotes we observe on television, online, and in our personal lives.

We humans need to use judgmental heuristics in our increasingly complex societies and so we use them without even realizing it. Whatever you thought might be credible laws depicted on television shouldn't be trusted. A repeated marathon of episodes in which fictional police only act positively towards the general public would cause an obvious bias with an implicit understanding that police are legally required to protect the public; it follows along the lines of the motto "protect and serve", it is what young children are

---

22. [64] Cialdini, Robert B. "Chapter 1: Weapons of Influence (1-16)" *Influence: Science and practice*. 4th ed., 21st Century Bks, 2002.

led to believe when meeting friendly police officers during their time in school, it follows the norms of what we expect when we see TV shows like COPS that selectively show favorable police chases, and the fact remains that it isn't legally accurate. US citizens don't have the right to police protection. What people have done is let the belief in symbols, the repeated exposure to favorable police shows, and the popular opinion of the public give them a misrepresentation of the actual law.[6566] In conjunction with mental shortcuts, the associations of symbolism with conceptual beliefs of what they represent by filling in the gaps of our knowledge with imagery that gives us a plethora of (usually positive) feedback loops is known as cognitive ease; that is, filling in our ignorance with concepts that feel familiar to us as a result of repeated exposure to the mental and emotional associations

---

23. [65] Kahneman, Daniel. Chapter 6:"Norms, Surprises, and Causes" (71-78). *Thinking, fast and slow*. Farrar, Straus and Giroux, 2015.

24. [66] Cialdini, Robert B. "Chapter 6: Authority (178-200)" *Influence: Science and practice*. 4th ed., 21st Century Bks, 2002.

they evoke in us.[67] Neither the fact that the majority of the 320 million people living in the US believe that police are legally suppose to protect citizens nor the fact that 320 million people are bombarded with imagery, symbols, and stories of police heroics make the law any less valid or impactful upon people's daily lives. If you believe that this is a lie then I encourage you to independently verify the lawful impact of "Castle Rock V. Gonzales" for yourself but I have provided the appropriate source in the citation of this book.[68] We humans have a tendency to go with information and repeated exposure to what is most available to us.[69] It is known as the availability bias within psychology and it is a psychological factor that governments, police

25. [67] Kahneman, Daniel. Chapter 5: Cognitive Ease (59-70). *Thinking, fast and slow*. Farrar, Straus and Giroux, 2015.

26. [68] No. 04-278 TOWN OF CASTLE ROCK, COLORADO v. JESSICA GONZALES. https://www.justice.gov/sites/default/files/osg/briefs/2004/01/01/2004-0278.mer.ami.pdf 1-45. Supreme Court of the United States. 27 June 2005.*Justice.Gov*. United States, 27 June 2005. Web. 5 Feb. 2018. <https://www.justice.gov/sites/default/files/osg/briefs/2004/01/01/2004-0278.mer.ami.pdf>.

27. [69] Kahneman, Daniel. Chapter 12: The Science of Availability (129-136). *Thinking, fast and slow*. Farrar, Straus and Giroux, 2015.

organizations, the national media, and psychologists are well aware of.

It is the same with religion. It shows that millions of people can wholeheartedly have an understanding about the norms of their society, harbor an overwhelmingly positive outlook on an organization and what it is perceived to do based on implicit understandings, and be completely wrong. You and others may already understand such a concept by acknowledging the billion of people who have strong religious faith in a religion different from yours. The fact that millions upon millions of people believe that police officers are legally required to protect them and this belief is what they consider to be a normal aspect of their everyday lives doesn't make the belief true.[70] If you were in a similar position to Gonzales and lost a loved one through police failure in doing their duty, your ignorance about this ruling would serve as a detriment to you. The police wouldn't need to pay any damages for failing you or

28. [70] Walton, D. N. "Appeal to Popularity." *Https://Www.logicallyfallacious.com*, www.logicallyfallacious.com/tools/lp/Bo/LogicalFallacies/40/Appeal-to-Popularity.

your loved one. At best, they would simply be forced into retirement. Your ignorance, created by an obfuscation of the real facts through positive cultural imagery, will be used against you. It is also important to consider how many of us come to these beliefs. We often observe and consider what other people think or do and copy that behavior in order to remain in a favorable view to the majority of people; that is known as social proof.[71] The majority of people being confronted with this legal fact might be skeptical and may view such a legal fact to be a conspiracy theory. After all, it doesn't follow any coherent understanding about their beliefs regarding American society and it doesn't fit a coherent expectation about US law itself.[72][73] Yet it is a real law, but accepting that would require a drastic change of

29. [71] Cialdini, Robert B. "Chapter 4: Social Proof (98-140)" *Influence: Science and practice*. 4th ed., 21st Century Bks, 2002.

30. [72] Kahneman, Daniel. Chapter 19: The Illusion of Understanding (199-208). *Thinking, fast and slow*. Farrar, Straus and Giroux, 2015.

31. [73] Kahneman, Daniel. Chapter 20: The Illusion of Validity (209-221). *Thinking, fast and slow*. Farrar, Straus and Giroux, 2015.

perception regarding what most Americans have come to expect regarding their own safety and the safety of their loved ones.

As mentioned earlier, you probably acknowledge that a billion of people believe in a religious faith that is different from yours. Currently, Christians make up the largest population in the world. In almost every country, there is at least a minority Christian population. For all the speeches about how India and China have a majority Hindu or majority atheist population, it remains true that Christianity – as a whole – has the largest population size.[74] Yet, this is not a valid argument favoring Christianity. This is what is known as the appeal to popularity fallacy. Consider this hypothetical argument: what if Judaism turned out to be the one true religion? If that were so, then it wouldn't matter how many people across the world believed in Christianity, it wouldn't even matter if every country in the world outside of Israel believed in Christianity. It wouldn't matter if every

32. [74] Hackett, Conrad, and David McClendon. "World's Largest Religion by Population Is Still Christianity." *Pew Research Center*, Pew Research Center, 5 Apr. 2017, www.pewresearch.org/fact-tank/2017/04/05/christians-remain-worlds-largest-religious-group-but-they-are-declining-in-europe/.

person in the world believed in Christianity while Judaism was no longer believed in. It would be meaningless in the face of Jewish people being the chosen people of God. You can substitute this proposition with another religion or reverse it; if Christianity is true then Jewish people have suffered throughout history for a meaningless cause or – worse still – they have endured suffering to be killed en masse for some apocalyptic prophecy. Now consider this: according to most recent polling data, Islam will be the world's largest religion by around 2030 - 2035.[75] If that prediction becomes true, then what value can there be in Christians making up the majority of the world population currently? It has no value and on closer inspection, it is less meaningful than most Christians might realize. Christianity has divided into Protestants, Catholics, East Orthodoxy, and a voluminous amount of other sects; in other regions of the world Christianity has blended with the local religions and changed. For example, Catholics of India follow a Caste system just

33. [75] "The Changing Global Religious Landscape." *Pew Research Center's Religion & Public Life Project*, Pew Research Center's Religion & Public Life Project, 26 July 2017, www.pewforum.org/2017/04/05/the-changing-global-religious-landscape/.

like the Hindus. In the Philippines, books of local religious witchcraft have been blended together with Christian teachings. There is no, and there probably will never be, a uniform Christianity; but this is not a unique problem to Christianity. It is the natural occurrence of any belief spreading. It is why India has had a tradition of Hindu heterodoxy, why Islam has differences in Sunni and Shia, and why there are intrinsic differences in several Buddhist schools of thought. In the context of the United States, liberals and conservatives have diametrically opposed views of Jesus Christ's teachings and expectations. What use is the term Christianity, or indeed any religious identity, when it has belief systems that conflict with each other on fundamental levels?

In chapter four, I will extrapolate on the faultiness of open interpretation and how all religions suffer from being unable to grapple with modernity.

Convenience

Religion has often been used to suit our conveniences. In the previous section, I mentioned how people living in first world countries ignore the circumstances of children in third world countries as having nothing to do with them and how religion helps ameliorate the immorality of such a position by the presumption of a positive afterlife for the children who have died. The death of innocent children is a regrettable truth that we should confront because it takes away the easiness and simplicity of religious answers. Religion, for the longest period of time, has helped facilitate apathy to problems of child mortality in third world countries but the apathy and convenience of religion doesn't end there.

The majority of people in any first world country don't give much thought to the problems of countries outside of theirs. Beyond selective media portrayals that create negative stereotypes, there is very little about foreign countries that most people understand and why should they? After all, it has little impact on their lives. As a result, due to our increasingly complex world and the shortcuts we use in understanding foreigners, we create negative stereotypes about other regions of the world and their people. Religion implicitly creates differences of in-group and out-group conditions and according to psychological research; the grouping of people into these different codifications is instantaneous.[76] *We group people into subjective categories instantaneously and sometimes we're not fully aware we act based on these subjective categories that we may hold to be self-evident truth.* We humans seem to be "groupist" by instinct from what extensive research has shown.[77] Race, religion, age, gender, political affiliation, citizenship, and other aspects of our personal identity have consequences for how we are all viewed by society. People codify us into groups, we codify them, and stereotypes are soon formed because of these rash generalizations from our "shortcuts" about other people.[78] This societal reality has a pernicious and demoralizing effect upon entire groups of people.

34. [76] Ispas, Alexa. "Chapter 1: Psychology and the Social Identity Perspective (1-24)" *Psychology and politics: a social identity perspective.* Psychology Press, 2014.

35. [77] Ispas, Alexa. "Chapter 2: The Psychology of Social Influence (26-50)" *Psychology and politics: a social identity perspective.* Psychology Press, 2014.
36. [78] McDermott, Rose. "Chapter 4: Cognition and Attitudes (77-117)" *Political*

In my discussions with fellow Millennials on facebook, in college clubs, and among friends; I would ask whether they noticed an implicitly racist codification conducted by the generations before us. Almost unanimously, the Millennials that I spoke with – among different social classes, having different racial backgrounds, and coming from different political affiliations – agreed with the strange behavior of the generations before us. What we all agreed on was thus: the older generation would assess the quality of an entire racial group by comparing the good and bad people of that racial group that they personally met. For my group of friends and I, this seemed both fundamentally absurd and stupid. By defining people by their racial group, you are erroneously attributing negative qualities to people who have nothing to do with each other beyond being born with the same skin pigmentation. This is fundamentally unfair and racist. To the keen observer, the argument from followers of this belief attributing these distinctions from the "good" or "bad" qualities of the racial "community" does little to obfuscate the underlying racism. A

Psychology in International Relations. Ann Arbor: U of Michigan, 2004. Print.

disturbing implication from this viewpoint is the ignorant idea that skin pigmentation is linked to bloodline. In online forums, people will speak of how racist family members of theirs will demand that certain other racial groups be kept out of their family line. However, if people believe that "race" has to do with one's familial blood then what these racists are advocating is incest. If they truly believe that skin pigmentation determines similarities in blood then this is an advocacy for certain degrees of incest. Fortunately, ignorant racists are entirely wrong; skin pigmentation was determined by people adapting to their specific climates in their environments and skin pigmentation is a phenotype and not homogenous ancestry. Thus, skin color has nothing to do with how genetically close you are to someone else. For example, if you're white, you may be closer in genetic relations to your fellow black members of society than your fellow white members. This is primarily because skin pigmentation is just one small part of our genetic make-up; these racial boundaries are a cognitive illusion fostered by misapplied cultural history and historic racism. Examples of this fact can be seen across the world: Northern

Indians of India are genetically closer to British people than Central and Southern Indians in genetic make-up most likely because of the Greco-Indian empire that rose after Alexander the Great's attempted conquest of India, most Europeans can trace their roots to the Near-East, Iraqis are classified as Caucasian and have a significant percentage of people who Westerners would classify as being "white", and Mexico has more diversity among different racial backgrounds than at first glance with White and Black "Hispanic" peoples. These distinctions are worthless anyway because the generalizations of each group are based on either racism or ignorant cultural discrimination. Generally speaking, racists have a difficult time classifying anything that isn't their expected similarity. The predominance of incestuous beliefs seems to be the root of most racism and this provincialism seems to be true of each country that practices it. I'd make the argument that US citizens are criticized for it because it is inconsistent with the championed diversity of the US and shows a failure of the education system of the US; furthermore, government codifications via racial background may be a double-edged sword because it promotes these implicit divisions by the evaluation of society through skin pigmentation.

During a news panel on Fox News in 2014, Megyn Kelly received a wide amount of criticism for saying to any possible children watching that Jesus Christ and Santa Claus were white.[79] After the public's derision of Kelly's statement, politicians ignored the part about Jesus Christ and shifted the focus to Santa Claus being a diverse cultural icon for children of all skin pigmentations. Virtually no politician or social media critic confronted the quirk about Jesus Christ being a white man and the backlash quickly died down. The educated members of the general public pointed out historical inaccuracies in social media regarding Jesus's skin pigmentation, groups of Christians stated that the skin color of Jesus Christ obviously didn't matter because his love for humanity is universal, and discussions about a black Jesus were largely met with an equal

---

37. [79] Merritt, Jonathan. "Insisting Jesus Was White Is Bad History and Bad Theology." *The Atlantic*, Atlantic Media Company, 12 Dec. 2013, www.theatlantic.com/politics/archive/2013/12/insisting-jesus-was-white-is-bad-history-and-bad-theology/282310/.

possibility to a white Jesus. This type of controversy over the racial background of a religious figure isn't unique to Jesus Christ or to religious discourse itself. Ancient stories about Cinderella, Ali Baba, and the 16 labors have changed a multitude of times to the renaming of the characters, the changes to the skin color of the characters, and the sanitization of the more morally dubious aspects of the stories that don't fit with the moral guideposts of the cultures that adopt the stories. In the context of religion, the Buddha has faced similar issues of cultural appropriation; his racial background has changed from Indian to the race of the majority population of each country that adapted Buddhism. In Korea, his appearance is reshaped to that of a Korean. In Taiwan, he looks Chinese; this is a blatant historical inaccuracy but these types of iconography persist throughout history and persist within each country where the majority of the population is of a different racial background from the revered figure. For the most part, within each country that Jesus and the Buddha are revered, their racial background changes to the majority population of that country. So, if the racial background of Jesus Christ and Gautama

Buddha don't matter then why does this form of cultural appropriation overwhelmingly persist throughout the world? A pernicious and unpopular answer could be our psychological biases; psychologists have found that human beings prefer to associate with others who are similar to them.[80] Psychologists have coined the term "relatedness" but from my studies in political psychology, I would argue that this terminology skims over the true impact of the meaning. A more appropriate term might be "narcissistic impulse" and each racial group's desire to praise their revered figure only under conditions in which the figure is depicted to have the same racial background as them. The persistence of these false depictions, which are historical inaccuracies, reveals each individual's narcissistic desire for their racial background to be the most important in the world. I suspect that it is an explicit and irrational form of religious convenience that isn't challenged because it would engender a surge of racism and hate speech from any group that faced such a challenge to their religious worldview. The iconography is more important to

_____

38. [80] Ispas, Alexa. "Chapter 2: The Psychology of Social Influence (26-50)" *Psychology and politics: a social identity perspective*. Psychology Press, 2014.

satisfying their narcissism than historical facts. While the socially progressive religious adherents are willing to acquiesce to the legitimate history of their religion, it would be more challenging to convince the more ignorant groups in any given country to do the same. This religious convenience reveals a schism of difference beyond the multitude of religious denominations that isn't discussed publicly. People remain silent about this global racist phenomenon throughout their religious practices precisely because challenging the issue would harm the convenience of the majority of religious people by forcing them to confront their inner narcissism.

Convenience and Coherence

In his best-selling book, *Thinking Fast and Slow*, Psychologist Daniel Kahneman unveiled the multitude of cognitive biases within the human psyche. One of these biases was our bias in framing events in the manner of storytelling. We create a coherent framework of the world through our own biased assessments and formulate our own causal relationships for why events happen.[81][82][83] Beliefs in a God

blessing us with good fortune is an example of finding a fanciful

cause for an event. Understanding this, Gods or God itself could be a

concept of convenience for humankind as a result of looking for the

"causes" of events through mental shortcuts. Examples can be seen in

every religion. In polytheism, different Gods serve different aspects of

human convenience from concepts such as a fountain goddess of luck

in Rome, to a goddess of love in Hinduism, to a God of trickery in the

Norse religion, to goddesses of death in Celtic religions, and to a God

of either love or torment who helps people in mysterious ways in the

Abrahamic faiths. The dualistic concept of God and the Devil are

ideological representations of Absolute Good and Absolute Evil. They

are depictions from the human mind's imagination, the justifications

for our actions, and come from our human biases to seek quick

---

39. [81] Kahneman, Daniel. Chapter 6:"Norms, Surprises, and Causes" (71-78). *Thinking, fast and slow*. Farrar, Straus and Giroux, 2015.

40. [82] Kahneman, Daniel. Chapter 7: A Machine for Jumping to Conclusions (79-88). *Thinking, fast and slow*. Farrar, Straus and Giroux, 2015.

41. [83] Kahneman, Daniel. Chapter 8: How Judgments Happen (89-96). *Thinking, fast and slow*. Farrar, Straus and Giroux, 2015.

answers to our grand world due to our desire for instant gratification. Due to the lack of technology and their lack careful assessment of the world around them by the majority of people in the ancient world, they sought stories and developed beliefs that satisfied their instant gratification in understanding the world around them.[84] They found links between actions and results that had no causal links like animal sacrifice and human sacrifice to change the weather patterns to keep their agricultural societies from starving or to provide a "cause" for why they were starving. They developed erroneous links because they needed quick and easily understood causes for why the world around them was a certain way depending on the time and place. It became understandable thanks to developing these Gods or God into teachings through storytelling to explain to themselves what they did right or wrong because the human mind is geared towards developing narratives to make sense of the world.[85]

---

42. [84] Nietzsche, Friedrich Wilhelm. "Aphorisms 40 and 41" *THE ANTICHRIST*. Translated by H. L. Mencken, The Project Gutenberg, 2006.

43. [85] Kahneman, Daniel. Chapter 19: The Illusion of Understanding (199-208). *Thinking, fast and slow*. Farrar, Straus and Giroux, 2015.

Our minds seek coherence in relation to stories we tell ourselves all the time. We use this framework of coherence in our understanding of history and the attachment we place upon historical figures that are similar to us; they help serve our desires for inspirational storytelling and our narcissistic impulse with how we draw similarities to them. An example of this is the stories of the Crusades. Depending on whether you are Christian or Muslim, you may attach yourselves to some of these heroic depictions in films, books, or television shows about the Crusades and liken yourself to one of the so-called heroes. But, were you aware that the ancient Christian factions practiced cannibalism during the time period of the Crusades?[86] Were you aware that a subset of Christians ate the people that they killed – including children? The censoring of this significant historical fact displays a chief problem with religion. Similar to the apathy of first world peoples to the plight of the third world, religious people ignore the horrific acts in the name of religion for the sake of

44. [86] Rubenstein, J. "Cannibals and Crusaders." *French Historical Studies*, vol. 31, no. 4, Jan. 2008, pp. 525–552., doi:10.1215/00161071-2008-005. PDF.

their own convenience. They ignore the barbarity to defend the view of religion being morally good for people. The negative history of their religion impacting the world is argued to be causes other than their religious teachings: the evil nature of humanity, the evil of politics, the instigation of the enemy, the mysterious will of God, and a multifarious amount of other supposed causes. Typically, the popular justification is that false interpretations of the faith occur and cause violence. It is an appeal to purity, an attempt at defending some perceived special and unique goodness of the religious faith. Apologists are willing to downplay, disingenuously interpret, and vilify attempts at highlighting horrific acts in the name of religion; to the extent that they ignore ongoing human rights crimes, ignore the victims of the past because they harm the positive coherence of religion, and may even come-up with a convenient notion that the victims are in a better place in the afterlife regardless of what the victims suffered. The lives and deaths of others become an abstract concept instead of a real event that has hurt real people. The notion of victims finding peace in the afterlife only serves the convenience and narcissism of the religious believer.

Criticisms of the religion itself can be obfuscated and ignored through the cognitive dissonance and the convenience of certain religious principles. The argument from ignorance that God's plan is unknowable serves the convenience of the religious adherent to ignore human rights abuses. Some religious believers try to detach themselves entirely from their previous religious identity; often by arguing that their faith isn't truly a religion and that they're simply spiritual without identifying with the religious identity because of the negative connotations associated with it. This is consistent with the psychological act of substitution, in which people find alternative reasons to justify their beliefs or actions because of unwillingness to change. Instead of dealing with a harsh self-critique in the face of new evidence about ones beliefs, people substitute analyzing a criticism with how that criticism makes them feel.[87] Instead of critically

---

45. [87] Kahneman, Daniel. Chapter 9: Answering an Easier Question (97-107). *Thinking, fast and slow*. Farrar, Straus and Giroux, 2015.

examining a belief based on a genuine criticism from an opposition group, they act on behalf of their personal feelings towards the criticism. Thus, they may not even concern themselves with the subject of human rights abuses by a religious organization they're affiliated with.

It isn't a morally good position because it reveals an apathetic disposition for the victims because victims are part of the out-group. To that end, people are self-centered because they are far more willing to ignore the victims for the sake of arguing for the purity of the religious faith. People simply don't care because they're unwilling to inconvenience themselves by examining their own beliefs. The result is an attempt to disassociate from the negativities while holding the exact same religious beliefs. The obfuscation and self-centeredness doesn't exist strictly for religion; it can exist in lesser known cultural forms but it is most damaging in the context of religion because of how easily people ignore human rights abuses because it doesn't fit into the positive image that they have about their own religious beliefs or those of their loved ones. They instead perceive it as a personal identity that "never leaves them" and the resulting trust in religious institutions or religious beliefs can have harmful effects upon people as a result.

The Convenience of Good and Evil

The dualistic concept of good and evil creates a limiting and damaging worldview that ultimately harms people who believe it to be the truth; even the idea that there are small gray areas in a mostly good and evil framework is harmful because it is an oversimplification. The concept of good and evil – above all other concepts – leads to extremism, xenophobia, bigotry, hatred, and mass murder. That may seem like an outrageous claim but I think it is truly an accurate assessment and here is why:

The dichotomy of Good versus Evil is extremist by default. It makes an extreme claim about our side and an opposing side. It implies the vast majority of a particular group are purposefully desiring wanton harm of our side while also implying that our side is an absolute good in the world. It defends any violence on "our side" in terms of the situation or for the greater good of our defense while the opposing side is using violence simply because they're "evil" or gullible people manipulated by evildoers in power. It imposes an absolutist metric upon vast swathes of people that codifies them all in an oversimplification instead of considering the situations from the opposing point of view. Even worse, it does little to differentiate people in foreign countries by political leanings, socio-economic leanings, and other multitudes of factors. After all, why should we believe there is a massive uniformity in another country and that they don't have class structures, political and social differences, and religious divisions that are worth considering when making a judgment about another country? The concept of Good versus Evil frames groups into absolutes and when people look for a "balanced" approach to important issues, we may be willing to concede that the opposing side has some good people that are mostly overshadowed by an abundance of evildoers; we also may concede that there are wrongdoers on "our side" but that the vast majority of our in-group are doing positive work. In short, seeing two opposing absolutes with a few shades of grey is generally the view from people who believe in good and evil. What people are doing is anchoring absolutes upon a general population of a particular country; instead of assessing them based on objective facts, we assess them based upon negative headlines and make spurious assumptions about the personalities of millions or perhaps billions of people based upon a single news story of a tragic event. By following this approach of instant gratification towards negative depictions of people in the news, we don't consider factors such as the differences in crime rates throughout a foreign country's cities versus its rural areas, lack of education such as illiteracy, and other socio-economic factors. Instead, we impose upon an entire country a stereotype by anchors. In psychological studies, the anchoring effect is setting a particular value based upon useless or erroneous information included in what a person sees when making a judgment on a value.[88] This typically relates to mathematical questions, but could relate to our moral judgments when using the

---

46. [88] Kahneman, Daniel. Chapter 11: Anchors (119-128). *Thinking, fast and slow*. Farrar, Straus and Giroux, 2015.

Good versus Evil perspective due to anchors being so ubiquitous in human behavior. In effect, people would be imposing a blanket extreme upon an entire country instead of assessing their pros and cons.

The Good versus Evil viewpoint isn't an objective reality, but rather a self-fulfilling prophecy. Consider this hypothetical idea: two nation-states are opposed to each other and they both believe in a strict viewpoint of good versus evil. Both sides see themselves as morally good and the opposing side as morally evil; they may concede that some small portions of their side behave wrongfully and that some good people exist on the other side but generally speaking, they oppose each other on strict moral beliefs by viewing the other side as mostly evil. What would relations between these two countries be like? It shouldn't be difficult to immediately grasp that both sides would be committing bloodbaths against each other on the basis of fighting evil, upholding the good morals of their society, and believing they're "doing what must be done" to protect themselves in defense of their country. After all, if you believe that the opposing side is pure evil, why bother negotiating? Or upon the pretense of negotiating, why bother upholding any concessions if you assume the opposing side is deceiving you constantly? As I see it, this "balanced" approach of Good versus Evil isn't balanced at all; for most countries and people, there is no good or evil with a few shades of grey that produce moral quandaries. There is only grey; there is only the moral quandaries. What people are doing is instead of looking at pros and cons of a country, individually assessing them based upon measures of human rights and political freedoms for example, they simply assume the majority of an entire country is full of good or bad actors who collectively seek either friendship with us or annihilation of us. This is obviously due to our mental shortcuts as we can't assess each nation-state individually. Sadly enough, we get negative viewpoints and form bigoted stereotypes because of streams of negative news about other countries and the vice versa is also possible. But what about truly extreme cases such as dictatorships like North Korea and absolute monarchies like Saudi Arabia? Well, there is a paradox to those examples: the people in those societies may see themselves as morally good and anything that disagrees with them as morally evil. Whether because of nationalistic fervor and lack of education in the case of North Korea or especially religious authoritarianism in the case of Saudi Arabia, people see themselves as being part of the moral good for strictly obeying what the religious bodies of the government or the single political party refers to as an absolute moral good because of their lifelong indoctrination. The addition of social proof, of seeing everyone in your environment behave with admiration and fealty to the leaders, will only further condition a person to seeing the teachings of the ruler as a foundation of moral good. In short, they unthinkingly believe themselves to be morally good because that's how they're brought up. Their belief in their culture's moral goodness leads to truly horrifying actions in what they perceive to be defense of the sacred beliefs of their society that appear to be morally evil to us in the outside world.

The dualistic concept of "Good versus Evil" is a framework and promotion of extremist ideology; the idea that it is a safe concept for children is false because of its extremist viewpoint. It is a concept that often compels people to hate and murder under a veneer of justice. Our groupist mentality intermingles with the extremist ideology of absolute good and absolute evil. Even the idea of mostly good or mostly evil is self-damaging because people have anchored their viewpoints upon the idea of absolute good and evil and given small concessions to what is still largely an absolutist disposition. Essentially, people will concede that some or a few good people exist on the opposing side and grant that some or a few people with violent tendencies exist within our side, but will remain firm in their generalizations that the majority of our side has heroic and humanistic qualities that justify our violent atrocities and that the other side commits violent atrocities due to the majority of them harboring stereotypical "evil" qualities like hatred for others or that they feel pleasure in committing violence similar to a cartoon super villain. In short, good and evil are recognized as being the only measure for an organized group of people to judge them. When we apply these dual extremist ideologies to our fellow human beings that are different from us then we will always be generalizing them with a simplistic worldview. There are different degrees of how pernicious this concept is but the problem is the concept itself being flawed and instigating hatred toward others. Viewing our moral beliefs as a form of goodness and viewing those opposed to our moral beliefs – such as in the abortion debate – as evil will create a dehumanizing image of the people who disagree with our views.

Apologists of the dualistic concept of good and evil are quick to point out truly horrific crimes as proof that the concept itself has merit. Common examples are the Holocaust, an anecdotal account such as the gruesome death of a child at the hands of a pedophile, or terrorism. Yet, upon a deeper look, these show a shallow understanding of the consequences of believing in good and evil. The Nazis committed a mass genocide after a voluminous amount of religious and political propaganda condemning the Jews for being evil people throughout the history of Christian Europe. The Nazis used the economic crisis, the belief that the Jews were responsible for murdering Jesus Christ, and anecdotal stories to argue that Jewish people were a villainous and hateful group that ruined their country.

The narrative of doing what must be done to protect the innate goodness of the German people was used to instill the idea that German soldiers were heroically going through hell and committing these atrocities to protect the goodness of the German public. That was the basis for the Holocaust, the belief that the Germans were truly good people who needed to destroy the evil of the world and that meant killing the Jews because they personified evil for the Nazis. A violent pedophile who made a child suffer usually emphasizes their other actions, such as giving to charity, to ameliorate themselves from their horrific sexual tendencies; the pedophile vindicates themselves of responsibility by telling themselves that they're mostly a good person. How can we know this? Because that is exactly what the national media does to protect their image and many pedophiles wearing religious garb had defenders who blamed the victims or found examples of a priest being a "good person" to vindicate their rape of children. Psychologists have found that most terrorists, by and large, aren't insane extremists. While some terrorists like the al Qaeda hijackers show a lack of ability to distinguish religious beliefs from reality; shockingly, some terrorists such as the Irish Republican Army are people who turned to violence after seeing their efforts through more peaceful means being ignored or violently crushed – such as peaceful protests or the judicial system being purposefully ineffectual.[89] A terrorist would argue the innate goodness of their actions or possibly highlight how the foreign country that they're trying to destroy committed more egregious acts of violence upon their people to justify their behavior. In fact, that has been done in the case of Iraqi insurgents; they justified the beheadings by blaming President Obama for beginning an initial bombing campaign that Wall Street and the US's Gulf allies demanded of him to protect global economic interests. We have known instances of terrorists justifying their violence through the concept of good and evil; Osama bin Laden's letter to America attempts to vindicate his terrorism as a form of heroics and posits the US as an empire of evil.[90]

---

47. [89] McDermott, Rose. Chapter 5: Do Actions Speak Louder Than Words? (119-152). *Political Psychology in International Relations*. Ann Arbor: U of Michigan, 2004. Print

48. [90] "Full text: bin Laden's 'letter to America'." *The Guardian*, Guardian News

In the case of the average person, good and evil thinking seems to lead people to believe in a "Good Person Syndrome" to self-exalt ourselves and other people that we believe to be in our in-group. Unsurprisingly, we ascribe villainous characteristics to a perceived hostile out-group. People living under the belief system of good and evil typically perceive themselves to be a "good person"; we, the in-group, thoughtlessly purchase cheap consumer commodities such as clothing made from Chinese sweatshops, jewelry that was found from child labor in India, the latest electronic gadgets that were made from factories that force workers in third world countries into long hours while paying their workers pennies a day, oil from the dictatorships of OPEC, and when confronted with any of these realities then we argue that we're good people because of the positive relationships that we have in our personal lives. We argue that we're a good mother, a good father, a good spouse, a good friend, and give to a few charities. We say that evil is just part of how the world exists. We don't try to inconvenience ourselves or admit to profiting off the suffering of the

and Media, 24 Nov. 2002,
www.theguardian.com/world/2002/nov/24/theobserver.

third world because it enriches our lives. Attempts at pointing this out lead to a backlash of calling out hypocrisy from those highlighting these issues, or blaming the out-group by arguing their governments and therefore the victims themselves are responsible. This is despite the fact that some of these victims live under authoritarian rule or have no means of defending themselves. Once blaming the victim is accomplished, the Good Person Syndrome makes itself content by arguing perspectives of self-worship. Utilizing arguments such as how we treat our in-groups civilly, how our in-group is more civilized and open than the out-group through anecdotal evidence presented in the national news media to promote jingoism and confirmation bias used from the media, and ignore or distance ourselves from these realities by arguing that we're a humble folk who have nothing to do with the complexities of the world. Evidently, once there are moral questions that cannot be answered, a believer of good and evil will always argue that they are less than the complexity of the world and that these issues are "greater than themselves"; they ignore the fact that these questions would require them to rid themselves of their convenient, enriched lifestyle and they attribute negative qualities to vilify the people who point out these challenging questions. This isn't because they are secretly horrible people or because of some evil nature in humanity; it is because they wish for their lives to have a coherent and largely positive narrative. To effectively have a positive worldview when believing in the extremist ideology of good and evil, they need to ignore the terrible exploitation or find "causes" for what their belief system teaches them is evil in the world. We humans have a negativity bias and negative information is more difficult to get rid of than positive information.[91] Yet, it remains true that this dualistic and extremist teaching serves to create impotence towards complex problems in human affairs and leaves young people unable to deal with the real world.

The psychological effects known as the contrast principle and the consistency to an in-group play a significant role. Psychologists have noted, and national news media has taken advantage of, the fact

---

49. [91] Kahneman, Daniel. Chapter 28: Bad Events (300-309). *Thinking, fast and slow*. Farrar, Straus and Giroux, 2015.

that people put more emphasis on contrasting characteristics than what is necessarily there when we observe two different groups or arguments from opposing sides of a subject.[92] The contrast principle can apply to people, expensive items, political ideologies, and many other things. Psychologists have also noted that most people don't have the time or they're disinclined to take the effort in assessing each event respectively and instead choose to automatically respond with their prior behavior and social identity to the particular issue.[93] An example of the news taking advantage of these two psychological principles would be Piers Morgan, a US news reporter, interviewing Alex Jones, a conspiracy theorist, when his viewership was low on CNN.[94] Morgan's arguments would obviously look more favorable compared to that of a conspiracy theorist. Viewers comparing Morgan to a loudmouth who wasn't making much intelligible sense would

50. [92] Cialdini, Robert B. "Chapter 1: Weapons of Influence (1-16)" *Influence: Science and practice*. 4th ed., 21st Century Bks, 2002.

51. [93] Ispas, Alexa. "Chapter 2: The Psychology of Social Influence (26-50)" *Psychology and politics: a social identity perspective*. Psychology Press, 2014.

52. [94] Morgan, Piers. *YouTube*, CNN, 7 Jan. 2013, www.youtube.com/watch?v=ror9v2LwHoY.

further emphasize Morgan's positive qualities by a quick comparison of the two. Furthermore, viewers would likely feel that Piers Morgan was a reasonable person with common sense like them making him part of their "in-group" of "reasonable people" and would contrast that with Alex Jones who would be viewed as a crackpot. Unless the viewership is predisposed to Alex's views, they would overwhelmingly see the positive aspects of Piers Morgan because of the contrast to someone perceived to be a worse person. Incidentally, the contrast principle is probably why Godwin's law, reductio ad Hitler, is used in so much in Western social media to defend poor arguments or to emphasize the bad qualities of an opponent's arguments. Let's face it, virtually any action or argument looks better in contrast to a mass genocide by a genocidal and racist maniac.

Good and evil creates a grotesque oversimplification and anchors good and evil caricatures similar to cartoon characters onto real human beings. Instead of assessing events, peoples, places, or opposing arguments as their own individually; good and evil creates an anchoring effect. We already have the perception that a person's argument is "good" or "bad" based on how closely we perceive their views to be similar to ours or how we feel about what the subject that will be argued. Good and evil frames individual concepts with a favorable or antagonistic predisposition before people have made arguments. It typically describes out-groups as mostly evil compared to the in-group that is making the assessment. People with opposing views to the in-group are presumed to be liars, charlatans, idiots, or other nefarious connotations before we actually take the time to understand their views. We would also be predisposed to viewing egregious acts – even criminal acts – by people we like to be irrelevant. Even when they have committed a horrific act, it may be ignored or downplayed, simply because we believe them to be good based on how similar their views are to ours. While the dualistic belief doesn't always result in this, it is more likely because of the framework of good and evil.

Good and evil becomes dangerous when it leads to generalizations of entire peoples; these generalizations serve to create narratives similar to children's fantasy books about the real world.

We, as a culture, give ourselves narratives of self-exaltation of good and championing the good of the world, while presuming nefarious or evil intent from all others different from us.[95] We would be predisposed to assume evil intent on the part of other countries and peoples; this is especially true when the rational reasons for events are absent. When we have no rational basis for our understanding of why events happened – such as war, police taking down protests, or terrorist attacks – then we presume that the other side has an evil intent because that is the coherent framework of good and evil. Worse than that, good and evil is a concept that is averse to listening to rational discourse; the basic premise of the concept is that we must stand for the good and that means celebrating our peoples and cultures as morally or economically superior to the evil Other.[96] The need for coherence in our minds would presume evil intent on the part of others for their actions and the externalizing of evil then compels us

---

53. [95] Hedges, Chris. *War Is a Force That Gives Us Meaning*. PublicAffairs, 2002.

54. [96] McDermott, Rose. *Political Psychology in International Relations*. Ann Arbor: U of Michigan, 2004. Print. For reference: Chapter 4: Cognition and Attitudes (77-117)

to frame racist, bigoted, and hateful narratives because those people are different from us.[97] The lack of a rational basis for events makes it easier for people to hate others under the framework of good and evil. The inculcated framing of entire groups of people as "the other" through national news media's use of anecdotal evidence then compels us to conduct war or mass violence. It isn't just bigoted framing, but distancing to create a gap between the "good" people and the "evil" people, terms such as "foreign nationals", "Hajis", "Dykes", "illegals", "aliens", and other such terms create this implicit and psychological distance to form dehumanization campaigns. An important part of this that politicians, journalists, and psychologists understand about the general public, is that when you aren't given rational reasons for why an event happens then you will find your own "causes" to form a coherent narrative because every human being needs a coherent understanding of the world around them to both maintain a sense of control and to reduce personal anxiety over dangerous events.

---

55. [97] Hedges, Chris. *War Is a Force That Gives Us Meaning*. PublicAffairs, 2002.

The 2015 Baltimore riots serve as an important example; many detractors blamed the "thug culture" of young black Americans as the basis for the riots. This is an erroneous claim for most open-minded peoples; rap music isn't going to compel people to act differently than what they already were inclined to do. The true cause of the riots were Baltimore police's brutality of the civilian populations; there were mass settlements amounting to 5 million per year to settle cases of police brutally assaulting civilians – in one case, the police assaulted a pregnant woman.[98] Baltimore citizens were appealing to their government and demanding legitimate change for over five years but absolutely nothing was done. Upon agreeing to the settlements for family members who were hospitalized from police brutality, the civilians were legally obstructed from bringing these instances of police violence to the national news media. As a result, the national news media was able to frame a very one-sided narrative. While it is true that crime is a problem in Baltimore, the local government and the national news media have simply obstructed and

---

56. [98] Puente, Mark. "Sun Investigates: Undue force." *The Baltimore Sun*, 28 Sept. 2014, data.baltimoresun.com/news/police-settlements/.

ignored the suffering of the residents. But do you see how shallow framing this issue in terms of good and evil is? The national news media isn't entirely wrong about gang violence and the crime rates of Baltimore but they ignored the average citizen being brutally attacked by police officers to give a slanted view of what was the true cause of those riots. The burning down of shops, more often than not, was because of opportunistic anarchists from outside of the area coming in to destroy property; this was true for both Ferguson and Baltimore but the belief in "thug culture" created a racist predisposition that made people believe that black Americans just wanted to burn down their own cities to riot.

The good and evil framework for determining moral actions has a deeply pernicious social consequence that every human civilization has probably conducted during its history. The historical revisionism of civilian deaths in wars, the historical revisionism of genocides conducted upon perceived out-groups of peoples and the total apathy for civilian victims because they're perceived as the enemy come from the purview of good versus evil. Generally, the people of the nation-state that caused egregious war crimes and genocide argue that the human rights crimes don't matter. This is the cruelest degree of apathy for the victims who suffered and is principally argued from the perspective of viewing the victims as abstract concepts instead of viewing them as fellow human beings. The lives of in-groups, people who share our background, are more important than the out-groups, the foreign civilians who we generalize through our rash judgments. Cultural self-worship lead to venerating our positive qualities and trying to find "moral equivalence" with our nation-state's crimes and the crimes of people within their group either conducted upon us or conducted upon their civilians. Differentiating different political groups, differentiating the terrorist groups from the civilians, and attempting to condemn all atrocities on the religious basis of murder being wrong are ignored. The only genocides denounced as wrongful acts are those that help create national unity, celebrate the nation-state as the greatest force of good, and highlight anecdotes of soldiers saving civilians. Genocides that our nation-state conduct upon others are disingenuously misrepresented; the genocides are downsized in their actual impact, blame is thrown upon the victims or their governments while ignoring our government's culpability, a negative social custom of theirs is highlighted to justify genocide, it is sometimes argued that bringing it up is unpatriotic and somehow an insult to our nation-state's troops, and most people of the aggressor nation-state argue that it doesn't matter. Revisionist history removes the genocide from their textbooks and usually racist caricatures of the "enemy" nation-state are formed or heavily implied from grade school textbooks. A prominent example of this is the genocide of approximately 500,000 Iraqis – most of them 5 year old children – via the unilateral sanctions of the United States upon Iraq under the policy of Dual Containment.[99]

Genocide denial is probably the most disgusting and egregious crime that any human civilization can do upon other human civilizations. It emphasizes dehumanization, it ignores the lives of victims as less important than feeling good about celebrating the

---

57. [99] Gause, F. Gregory . "Getting It Backward on Iraq." *Foreign Affairs*, Foreign Affairs, 28 Jan. 2009, www.foreignaffairs.com/articles/iraq/1999-05-01/getting-it-backward-iraq.

nation-state, and it misapplies the blame for the crimes. It is not the civilians, but the terrible actions of the government that is being blamed for policy directives that purposefully resulted in mass death. Why should the civilians feel insulted or feel responsible? Acknowledging human rights crimes during war and crimes of genocide are just an acknowledgement that the lives of the victims had intrinsic value because they were innocent human beings. People don't fathom being on the opposite end of the debate. Yet, throughout human history, religion - the so-called epitome of good moral teachings - constantly fails to breed empathy for perceived out-groups even when children are dying or killed. Often, religion simply justifies or excuses human violence with religious precepts. This will be covered more in-depth in Part II.

Apathy and Silence towards Warfare

One of the greatest challenges, and least discussed topics, against religious faith is how shallow these so-called moral convictions truly are when jingoism sets in to begin war against a foreign entity. The sad fact of life is that war propaganda is successful in instilling hatred, racism, bigotry, and a desire for warfare against foreign countries. If morality truly was an important component of our existence then why does it become drowned away when a government prepares itself to launch a war campaign? This is essentially true for every country in the world; at some point, your country went to war and morality went to sleep. Notice that religious organizations of countries launching wars will always become silent about the morality of killing during times of war. They will almost unanimously grow silent in any moral objections. Worse still, average citizens will ignore the war crimes, bombings of foreign civilian homes, and largely create a fictitious understanding of warfare to praise their soldiers as humane when they conduct night raids, bomb houses, kill civilians, and – in some cases – rape civilians. The narrative of good and evil takes a strong hold to make the other side similar to the boogeyman to justify war – i.e. to justify organized mass murder.[100] Foreign civilians are always caught in the crossfire; through two sides shooting at each other or through bombing

---

58. [100] Hedges, Chris. *War Is a Force That Gives Us Meaning*. PublicAffairs, 2002.

campaigns. A nation-state always ignores or drowns out the civilian killings committed by their soldiers. The afterlife, the idea of a Higher Power's plan, and other abstract concepts become excuses to ignore such barbarity.

How can we explain this nigh-universal cognitive dissonance in morality? Why do citizens of all countries have apathy towards their country committing war crimes? Where is the moral condemnation when it truly matters? It is simple: it suits our convenience as an in-group; when people aren't being forced into conscription and aren't personally affected by something then they simply won't concern themselves with the issue. For the most part, people pay attention to their immediate surroundings and daily routine – soldiers committing war atrocities upon innocent civilians in another country is equivalent to changing weather forecasts on the news. People simply don't care; religious beliefs – when they are truly needed – are met with intense social apathy and usually ignorance of the political events in question. That is the reality of how most people practice their religious faith. Jingoism wins and trumps religious morals. Usually religion blends with racial or cultural jingoism to defend wars and ignore war atrocities; what use is morality in these repeated scenarios?

Consequently, we differentiate killings during war from murders within our countries. This isn't simply true of soldiers battling combatants, this is also true in the case of soldiers slaughtering an entire village of civilians – such as in the Haditha killings.[101] Why? A possible utilitarian reason is this: the nation-state differentiates killing in the name of obtaining a political or economic objective (which maximizes State power) versus killing people within the country. Killing people within the country is an act that weakens State power because the murdered individual is useful human capital and further weakens the strength of a nation-state should such acts go ignored because people of similar ethnocentric, gender, sexual orientation, or political background will want equal treatment for their group. The people similar to the victim will demand punishment for

59. [101] Pelley, Scott. "Haditha massacre defendant: We did what we had to." *CBS News*, CBS Interactive, 6 Jan. 2012, www.cbsnews.com/news/haditha-massacre-defendant-we-did-what-we-had-to/.

the murder committed. Incidentally, in the case of Haditha – and almost all other instances in which soldiers have massacred foreign civilians – the Good Person Syndrome takes full effect; the murdering of children, the handicapped, and other foreign civilians are wholly ignored whilst news media runs stories about how the soldier, usually a man, is a family man with children and a wife. The paradigm of good and evil sets in and the most inconsequential displays of the abstract "goodness" of the soldier are trumpeted while the heinous deed is ignored.[102] Thus, the soldier faces no jail time and is still allowed to live a normal life within the country. Usually the story is never editorialized again because it hurts the coherence of their country being a force of good that the majority of people believe about their country.

This is not meant to be snarky and I didn't single out an example from the United States to insult it; I'm simply pointing out a modern example of a realistic fact about all nation-states. The late 19th

---

60. [102] CHEDEKEL, LISA , et al. "Haditha: Marine Linked To Civilian Deaths Was A Quiet Honor Student, Friends Say." *Hartford Courant*, 3 June 2006, articles.courant.com/2006-06-03/news/0606030586_1_frank-wuterich-haditha-squad-leader.

and earliest 20th century were probably the worst periods of war, genocide, and human rights crimes in terms of scope and scale. This example is simply meant to convey an evident fact: good and evil doesn't work and results in ignoring morality over providing positive moral answers to the most important questions. It is limiting, shallow, and makes people confused and disoriented in understanding real life events. In Part 2, I will elaborate my contentions on specific religions and why they cause pro-war narratives that result in mass death. However, before that, there are still other general issues of religious faith that will be covered.

Chapter 2: Asceticism and Rationality

"If we leave aside the ascetic ideal, then man, the animal man, has had no meaning up to this point. His existence on earth has had no purpose. "Why man at all?" was a question without an answer. The will for man and earth was missing. Behind every great human destiny echoes as refrain an even greater "in vain!" That's just what the ascetic ideal means: that something is missing, that a huge hole surrounds man. He did not know how to justify himself to himself, to explain, to affirm. He suffered from the problem of his being. He also suffered in other ways: he was for the most part a sick animal. The suffering itself was not his problem, but rather the fact that he lacked an answer to the question he screamed out, "Why this suffering?" Man, the bravest animal, the one most accustomed to suffering, does not deny suffering in itself. He desires it, he seeks it out in person, provided that people show him a meaning for it, the purpose of suffering. The curse that earlier spread itself over men was not suffering, but the senselessness of suffering—and the ascetic ideal offered him a meaning!

The ascetic ideal was the only reason offered up to that point. Any meaning is better than no meaning at all. However you look at it, the ascetic ideal has so far been a "faute de mieux" [for lack of something better] par excellence. In it suffering was interpreted, the huge hole appeared filled in, the door shut against all suicidal nihilism. The interpretation undoubtedly brought new suffering with it—more profound, more inner, more poisonous, and more life-gnawing suffering. It brought all suffering under the perspective of guilt . . . But nevertheless, with it man was saved. He had a meaning. From that point on he was no longer a leaf in the wind, a toy ball of nonsense, of "without sense." He could now will something—at first it didn't matter where, why, or how he willed: the will itself was saved.

We simply cannot conceal from ourselves what's really expressed by that total will which received its direction from the ascetic ideal: this hate against what is human, and even more against animality, even more *against material things—this abhorrence of the senses, even of reason, this fear of happiness and beauty, this longing for the beyond away from all appearance, change, becoming, death, desire, even longing itself—all this means, let's have the courage to understand this, a will to nothingness, an aversion to life, a revolt against the most fundamental preconditions of life—but it is and remains a will! . . . And to repeat at the conclusion what I said at the start: man will sooner will nothingness than not will . . ."[103]* - Friedrich Nietzsche, *On the Genealogy of Morals.* Ian Johnston Translation.

Asceticism has existed multifariously throughout all religious traditions. Almost every religion, and especially modern religions, has theological teachings that infer practices that temper feelings of chasing after a fleeting happiness; religions claim to offer a tempering of selfishness, greed, envy, hatred, and jealousy. They contain teachings that practice the concept of modesty towards sexual conduct and preach of living for a higher purpose above purportedly base desires. Self-control is implied throughout these religious teachings. A benign detachment from emotions that cause negative feelings and negative responses are heavily inferred to be the best way to live a good life. Above all the negativities attached to all religions in our

---

1. [103] Nietzsche, Friedrich Wilhelm. *On the genealogy of morals: a polemical tract.* Translated by Ian Johnston, PDF, Richer Resources Publications, 2014.

modern times, this seems to be the genuine positive source of religious morality and teaches people to live ethically. Separated from mystical abstraction, this seems to be a positive guideline to most people.

I argue that these presumptions are utterly false. Asceticism doesn't have any positive moral guidelines; it doesn't instill people with any form of moral goodness and I would argue that all it does is try to escape from reality by positing a higher purpose of living beyond the world. For all intents and purposes, asceticism only accomplishes the following: *to practice impotence as a form of moral goodness*. Cloaked under a veneer of goodness and self-worship; asceticism teaches us to give up on personal dreams by asserting our goals are unattainable, asceticism offers the convenient narrative that we would be self-centered to aim for our dreams in life, the ascetic lifestyle instills us to pretend that we're above those who attain more than us, and we commit to this outlook through the concept of self-renunciation for a purported higher purpose.[104] The desire for accomplishment and success is categorized closely to having evil intent in a disingenuous representation of positive work ethics. Moreover, the ascetic ideal disproportionately focuses on all human flaws and utilizes the mere existence of flaws to condemn all forms of human progress as both self-centered and evil. A commitment to self-constraint by a religious group only further solidifies this in-group commitment to impotence and to view anyone with a positive work ethic as a negative out-group with selfish intent or foolish beliefs. This doesn't speak of every individual case, but a person's commitment to asceticism usually comprises of an aversion to desiring more from life. Selfishness is typically viewed as an anathema to a constricted form of equality under an ascetic outlook.

A Will to Nothingness

---

2.   [104] Nietzsche, Friedrich Wilhelm. *On the genealogy of morals: a polemical tract.* Translated by Ian Johnston, PDF, Richer Resources Publications, 2014.

Asceticism is self-contempt obfuscated by religious iconography and religious platitudes. Concepts such as detachment from suffering and original sin are a sanctified self-hate of the individual to celebrate impotence as the only solution. The ascetic frames everything else in the world as having lesser value than prostrating towards self-impotence; using anecdotes and filling their gaps in knowledge of out-groups by postulating an out-group's nefarious intent to do harm to the world as an excuse to continue renouncing themselves from life.[105] Typically, an ascetic may use negative portrayals of people seeking fame in celebrity culture or running a business like a corporation that they see from films or negative news media coverage to fill in the gaps of what an ascetic doesn't know about different business industries to generalize seeking fame and fortune as evil, selfish, or narcissistic. This personal view is often disingenuous and erroneous.

---

3.   [105] Kahneman, Daniel. Chapter 5: Cognitive Ease (59-70). *Thinking, fast and slow*. Farrar, Straus and Giroux, 2015.

The ascetic ideal usually consists of a patronizing attitude toward all forms of self-empowerment: the foremost is the hatred for desiring material wealth; wealth is seen as meaningless, morally evil, and condemned via the argument that it doesn't last forever. The ascetic viewpoint presumes that people who seek material wealth will never truly be happy; that materialists doom themselves to intense struggle and suffering for no reason, and argue that looking beyond material wealth will confer a higher quality of life. Yet, the appeal to asceticism posits the idea that ascetics should be celebrated for giving up on material wealth under the presumption that ascetics could have succeeded in higher forms of wealth but simply chose not to do it. Such arguments show the intrinsic narcissism of asceticism itself; presuming an ascetic could persist in difficult and complex jobs but simply chose to pursue a so-called higher purpose is an attempt at self-flattery. Furthermore, wealth is obviously not intrinsically evil; what matters is what one does with the wealth and empowering oneself by gaining wealth is a worthwhile accomplishment. Regardless of death, a wealthier person has typically surmounted more challenges and accomplished more in life than ascetic individuals especially if they run international organizations. An example would be the American billionaires who have committed themselves to donating the vast swathe of their wealth to end world poverty. What could an ascetic possibly accomplish compared to billionaires who finance ending malnutrition to prevent children throughout the third world from dying, providing proper medical vaccinations for children that protect them from curable diseases that would otherwise ravage areas with child mortality, systems like the Janicki Omniprocessor that utilize sewer sludge to turn into electricity for communities in Africa[106], and commit themselves to decreasing the level of world poverty to increase overall life expectancy of children in the most vulnerable and poorest regions of the world?[107]

---

4. [106] Gates, Bill. *YouTube*, Thegatesnotes, 5 Jan. 2015, www.youtube.com/watch?v=bVzppWSIFU0.

5. [107] Gates, Bill, and Melinda Gates. "Warren Buffett's Best Investment." *Gatesnotes.com*, Bill and Melinda Gates, 14 Feb. 2017, www.gatesnotes.com/2017-Annual-Letter.

The dualistic belief of good and evil worsens this hatred of material wealth; people inclined to asceticism use anecdotes of greedy people on the news as confirmation bias that anyone who seeks material wealth is evil. The good and evil paradigm creates externalized evil caricatures such as Right-wing ideologies of Ayn Rand, Right-wing politicians, and obfuscates genuine issues pertaining to lower economic classes learning to despise material wealth. The good and evil paradigm, conflated with asceticism being framed as morally good, fills in gaps of knowledge about the rich and the poor with fairytale caricatures.[108] The wealthy elite are evil, greedy, self-centered, bigoted, believe themselves to be superior to the middle class and poor, and apparently they all became wealthy with "daddy's money" meanwhile the poor are good, honest, hardworking, down on their luck, and have hope that life will get better. These are simply ideological fantasies created from asceticism intermingled with good and evil. People who believe them generalize an entire group of peoples regardless of race, gender, sexual

---

6.   [108] Kahneman, Daniel. Chapter 5: Cognitive Ease (59-70). *Thinking, fast and slow*. Farrar, Straus and Giroux, 2015.

orientation, religion, and political affiliation to make themselves feel better about having accomplished less in life. These stereotypes about the wealthy and poor are psychologically, mathematically, and scientifically wrong regardless of the bigoted preconceived notions that people have. Yet, the patronizing attitude of asceticism along with the mindset of good and evil create a coherent framework that persistently generalizes anyone who tries to financially empower themselves. It obscures and sanctifies what is little more than jealousy of the wealthy.

The second, and equally as important, form of self-contempt is the hatred for all forms of sexual love. There is an overwhelming amount of hatred for the human body in the majority of religions and especially in the Abrahamic faiths. The human body elicits disgust, shame, and guilt for natural biological and biochemical processes of sex and masturbation. Sexual intercourse is openly condemned as sinful despite our natural biological processes for reproduction. The majority of religions teach a hatred for self-pleasure by referring to masturbation as "dirty" despite it having positive health benefits and being a natural process.[109][110][111][112] Worse than that, the deeper that a person delves into ascetic ideologies of any religion then the deeper this aversion to life persists. To commit themselves to a so-called higher purpose, many ascetics from Catholic parishes, Buddhist monks, or equivalents in other religions have foregone having a family with a spouse and having children.[113] The decision to renounce having a family because of religious convictions shows an aversion to human life in all theistic backgrounds. It isn't always because they have no interest in attaining a spouse and children; it is usually their

7. [109] Viglianco-VanPelt, Michelle, and Kyla Boyse. "Masturbation." Edited by Jennifer Gold Christner, *University of Michigan Health System*, July 2009, www.med.umich.edu/yourchild/topics/masturb.htm

8. [110] "Masturbation Side Effects and Benefits." *Healthline*, Healthline Media, www.healthline.com/health/masturbation-side-effects.

9. [111] Cooper, Spring Chenoa, and Anthony J. Santellla. "Happy news! Masturbation actually has health benefits." *The Conversation*, 5 Dec. 2017, theconversation.com/happy-news-masturbation-actually-has-health-benefits-16539.

10. [112] "Masturbation | Get the Facts About Masturbation Health." *Planned Parenthood*, Planned Parenthood, www.plannedparenthood.org/learn/sex-and-relationships/masturbation.

11. [113] Nietzsche, Friedrich Wilhelm. "Chapter IX: Preachers of Death (50-52)" *Thus spake Zarathustra: a book for all and none*. Translated by Thomas Common, PDF ed., T. Common, 1908.

commitment to this idea of a higher purpose that they renounce having a family, renounce finding personal love, renounce self-pleasure as dirty, and renounce sexual love as vile.[114][115] Pornography is condemned through hostile personal attacks and there are attempts to conflate normal pornography with criminal behavior like child pornography in order to shame people by associating natural activities with criminal behavior. Under the guise of morality, religious asceticism condemns healthy and natural activities as disgusting and infers that such behavior is evil. It teaches people to constantly feel shame, guilt, and self-hatred for not being "pure" enough to condemn their natural instincts as human beings.[116][117][118][119]

12. [114] Nietzsche, Friedrich Wilhelm. "Chapter IX: Preachers of Death (50-52)" *Thus spake Zarathustra: a book for all and none*. Translated by Thomas Common, PDF ed., T. Common, 1908.

13. [115] "Masturbation | Get the Facts About Masturbation Health." *Planned Parenthood*, Planned Parenthood, www.plannedparenthood.org/learn/sex-and-relationships/masturbation.

14. [116] "Masturbation Side Effects and Benefits." *Healthline*, Healthline Media, www.healthline.com/health/masturbation-side-effects.

15. [117] Nietzsche, Friedrich Wilhelm. "Chapter IX: Preachers of Death (50-52)" *Thus spake Zarathustra: a book for all and none*. Translated by Thomas Common, PDF ed., T. Common, 1908.

The third form of self-contempt is the hatred of knowledge. There are a plethora of reasons given for the disposition that we humans are of lesser value than a higher power: that religious adherents subject themselves to rules from a higher power for something that is beyond human comprehension, that the horrific events of war and genocide are part of God's plan for some unknowable reason to humanity, and that humans should look beyond the materialism of the world to be part of something greater than themselves. To await an unassailable truth that the human mind is too limited to understand. This is an overwhelmingly self-deprecating mentality that treats a hatred for knowledge as having intrinsic moral goodness. The implications are that giving up knowledge to a higher power is the correct path to a great truth and that we should ignore all negative human affairs: war crimes, genocide, bombing campaigns,

---

16. [118] Viglianco-VanPelt, Michelle, and Kyla Boyse. "Masturbation." Edited by Jennifer Gold Christner, *University of Michigan Health System*, July 2009, www.med.umich.edu/yourchild/topics/masturb.htm

17. [119] Cooper, Spring Chenoa, and Anthony J. Santellla. "Happy news! Masturbation actually has health benefits." *The Conversation*, 5 Dec. 2017, theconversation.com/happy-news-masturbation-actually-has-health-benefits-16539.

and the suffering of the third world poor as having less value than this great truth. This framework of moral goodness solidifies these horrific events as afterthoughts, the real people suffering are treated as afterthoughts, and asserts impotence towards these complex issues as having more value than effectively stopping them from happening. Thus, instead of effectively dealing with these issues, this moral framework treats these occurrences as too complex for human understanding and responds by sanctifying impotence as an act of good morals for the convenience of the adherents. *Prayer itself is the ultimate practice of impotence as a form of moral goodness*. Feeling good about praying to God and leaving it up to God to handle important matters like natural disasters is to feel good about yourself for doing nothing. You expend no effort to alleviate suffering and instead feel good about yourself for not expending effort or monetary assistance under the convenient belief that an omnipotent creator will help others. Prayer may give you a sense of control for what feels like unpredictable events and it may make you feel good personally, but you're feeling good about doing nothing of value for those who are suffering. You've put your personal feelings above the suffering of others and treated them as afterthoughts if all you do is pray for them. Participating in vetted charities that seek specifically to ameliorate suffering or donating money to vetted relief organizations that seek to help people who are suffering does far more to help because you're taking actionable steps to serve a community in need by empowering the sincere responders. If this segment has motivated you to pursue charitable works or to spend your personal income on them, please be wary of nefarious charities and be sure to properly look into charities you're considering to donate your money towards. As is well known, even some famous charities like those conducted by the celebrity Mother Teresa have been unveiled to be scams that lie about where the monetary proceeds go to; the charitable donations that she acquired went to building Churches and not hospitals as was ostensibly implied by her volunteer work.[120] Other charities by Christian missionaries often celebrate the deaths of innocents as the

---

18. [120] Hitchens, Christopher. "Christopher Hitchens: Hell's Angel: Mother Teresa (English Subtitles)." *YouTube*, BBC News, 7 Jan. 2015, youtu.be/NK7l_IhtKNU.

righteous judgment of the Abrahamic God, attempt to forcibly convert people after a disaster with some attempts to isolate and target children in particular, refuse food and medical treatment for people bleeding and starving in front of them unless they convert, and openly celebrate the suffering of survivors right in front of them immediately after the survivors have lost loved ones.[121][122][123][124] This is not meant to discourage charities, but to impress upon people to please be wary and research the charities you're donating money towards. Religious organizations, particularly Christian and Islamic organizations, often

19. [121] Neelakandan, Aravindan. "Why No Outrage over Conversion of Tsunami Victims?" *Swarajya*, 29 Dec. 2014, swarajyamag.com/politics/why-no-outrage-over-conversion-of-tsunami-victims.

20. [122] "When Nepal Was Groaning in Earthquake, Christian Missionaries Were Shamelessly Selling Jesus." *OpIndia*, 4 May 2015, www.opindia.com/2015/04/when-nepal-was-groaning-in-earthquake-christian-missionaries-were-shamelessly-selling-jesus/.

21. [123] Gittleson, Wendy. "Christian 'Soul Vultures' Are Exploiting The Nepal Earthquake 'For Christ' (VIDEO)." *AddictingInfo*, 27 Apr. 2015, addictinginfo.com/2015/04/27/christian-soul-vultures-are-exploiting-the-nepal-earthquake-for-christ-video/.

22. [124] Neary, Sarah. "Forced to Convert: How American Missionaries Really Treat Indigenous Akha Children." *Intercontinental Cry*, IC, 23 Apr. 2013, intercontinentalcry.org/forced-to-convert-how-american-missionaries-really-treat-indigenous-akha-children/.

see suffering in opportunistic terms precisely to preach ascetic ideals related to their religion.

The hatred of knowledge results in a hatred for human progress itself; there is a deep and pernicious nihilism in the purview of asceticism. The ascetic views all forms of human progress and modernity; hospitals, educational institutions, technology, waterways, houses, sanitation facilities, vaccines, better food, light bulbs, and a multifarious amount of other modern conveniences as insignificant and argue it will perish in the wake of a great truth that humans will never be fully able to comprehend.[125] This mindset displays the self-deprecating mentality of asceticism. It is a hatred for all of the positive accomplishments of humanity. Regardless of the accomplishments, even space age accomplishments of putting a man on the moon or having a satellite survey Mars, asceticism will view it as insignificant. Human progress is viewed as worthless either because of religious axioms or for the sake of some bizarre hope for

---

23. [125] Nietzsche, Friedrich Wilhelm. *On the genealogy of morals: a polemical tract*. Translated by Ian Johnston, PDF, Richer Resources Publications, 2014.

the end of the world.[126] In some cases, it's a conflation of both reasons. This nihilistic outlook towards human progress comes from religious obfuscation in favor of valuing impotence; from tenants such as detachment, ideologies of good and evil, and a bizarre belief in a great truth that usually requires the end of the world in virtually all religious faiths.

Arguably, the worst part is that theologians and religious believers from both Western and Eastern cultures have shown that the obscurity of religion, the perception of ancient mystery, archaic and outdated writings, and the mysticism of theology is enjoyable to the majority of religious believers.[127] Thus, religious believers take pleasure in the argument from ignorance and feel sadomasochistic pleasure in their self-contempt. The idea of living for a higher purpose beyond human comprehension leads to a morbid pleasure through

24. [126] Nietzsche, Friedrich Wilhelm. *THE ANTICHRIST*. Translated by H. L. Mencken, The Project Gutenberg, 2006.

25. [127] Nietzsche, Friedrich Wilhelm. *On the genealogy of morals: a polemical tract*. Translated by Ian Johnston, PDF, Richer Resources Publications, 2014.

ignorant self-constraint imposed by theological teachings and practices. Religious speakers often appeal to willful ignorance of scientific studies by telling religious believers that not knowing has a higher purpose. Usually by ascetically arguing that the scientist is arrogant and that no human being can truly understand God's will. It is this gap in understanding theology that differentiates atheists from the pious because atheists have a desire for verifiable truths that are demonstrable. This belief in viewing the world as inherently valueless or without meaning, viewing life in a state of constant decay or moral decline, and preaching that people who don't accept this perception are fools compared to one's in-group is a form of nihilistic narcissism.[128] An in-group of religious adherents view the world as empty and use pejorative terms to devalue life itself by comparing it to an argument from ignorance in which something beyond is considered of far more value, but also beyond their own human comprehension. This is both anti-intellectual and self-congratulates an

---

26. [128] Nietzsche, Friedrich Wilhelm. *On the genealogy of morals: a polemical tract.* Translated by Ian Johnston, PDF, Richer Resources Publications, 2014.

in-group for the anti-intellectualism because it is seen as keeping strong faith in the group and keeping the community together based on the collective imagination of a social group via dogma instead of verifiable claims based on evidence.[129] Whereas those who don't submit to this in-group standard are seen as selfish or narcissistic for not praising and seeing everything as valueless and worthless compared to a perfect world after death, a perfect creator deity that gets to know upon death, or a spiritual journey after death; the in-group praises itself for doing nothing of value in the world. It is a worship of impotence and death, seeing all forms of life as inherently devoid compared to something beyond their understanding.[130] Joining the in-group that views the world in various forms of decline, decay, and death is met with wide praise within the in-group as the groupthink motivates self-congratulatory praise for doing absolutely

---

27. [129] Ispas, Alexa. *Psychology and politics: a social identity perspective*. Psychology Press, 2014.

28. [130] Nietzsche, Friedrich Wilhelm. Chapter XXVI: THE PRIESTS (88-91). *Thus spake Zarathustra: a book for all and none*. Translated by Thomas Common, PDF ed., T. Common, 1908.

nothing and calling themselves humble for doing nothing of value.[131] Feeling assured in mutual trust that it must be real because of the social proof that others in their immediate surroundings believe in it with strong convictions.[132] They don't think about the multitude of millions of other religious denominations within their own faith or the billions who believe in other religions with their own denominational differences and how the majority of them hold the same mutual trust based on social proof of their small communities and strong communal values within those communities.

The Masculinity of Asceticism

Asceticism has a long history of gender-specific characteristics; many forms of asceticism were geared toward the gender concept of masculinity. Hating their own emotions by trying to be detached, a disgust for emotions being a source of strength, not

---

29. [131] Ispas, Alexa. *Psychology and politics: a social identity perspective.* Psychology Press, 2014.

30. [132] Cialdini, Robert B. "Chapter 4: Social Proof (98-140)" *Influence: Science and practice.* 4th ed., 21st Century Bks, 2002.

falling for so-called feminine wiles, discriminating women by generalizing them to be more emotional than men, perceiving crying as shameful, and so-called thrill-seeking by putting themselves at risk of death is the culmination of a philosophy of self-hatred.

Manly culture is almost wholly opposed to being human; ignoring the instinct to self-preservation to encourage putting their lives in danger, ignoring biological drives of pro-creation by vilifying women as sluts for practicing sexual liberation, viewing the normal biological function of tears as being a form of weakness, and viewing "toughness" as being emotionless seems like social conditioning into becoming a sociopath. A person with this sort of worldview is probably more likely to commit violent suicide to complete the social conditioning of self-hatred and misanthropy when faced with difficult social situations. Perhaps that is why suicidal men in the US commit the act violently by jumping off tall areas or committing mass violence before committing suicide by killing themselves or through suicide by cop.[133] It is statistically more likely for men across the world to commit suicide and teaching them this form of self-hate could be the reason but scientific and psychological studies would need to be made to be sure.

Perhaps tellingly, most of the criticisms that anti-feminists make about the double standards imposed upon men came from a long history of male culture that precedes the 19th century. It is odd that they would condemn feminism but then agree with feminist precepts that masculine culture is largely unfair to men too. Yet, it is the stupidity of the ancient cultures that created these forms of so-called appropriate male behavior.

Antiquated Rationality versus Modern Rationality

The self-hate of religious faith goes further through ascetic ideology. Rationality itself is viewed as synonymous with evil. Many

---

31. [133] Freeman, Daniel, and Jason Freeman. "Why are men more likely than women to take their own lives?" *The Guardian*, Guardian News and Media, 21 Jan. 2015, www.theguardian.com/science/2015/jan/21/suicide-gender-men-women-mental-health-nick-clegg.

ancient philosophers throughout the entirety of Western culture held

this self-destructive and self-defeating view of rationality. Rationality

became synonymous with harming other peoples and projected a view

that there was an innate evil within humankind itself. Examples such

as getting ahead in the business world by "screwing" your teammates

are one of these generalizations. This viewpoint is the most self-

deluded viewpoint to ever be conceived by any culture. Modern

epistemological rationality has shown the view to be a self-destructive

falsehood; causing harm to others can only harm oneself because you

will have made an enemy or you would have spent resources

weakening others ability to progress by squandering yourself.[134] It is

fundamentally irrational because you gain nothing from harming

others and instead make enemies for yourself. Western faiths and, to a

certain extent, Eastern faiths have a staunch self-defeating view of

rationality and logic existing within such a self-destructive context.

Intelligence is often viewed as utilizing evil intent and committing

32. [134] Yudkowsky, Eliezer. "What Do We Mean By "Rationality"?" *Less Wrong*, 16 Mar. 2009, lesswrong.com/lw/31/what_do_we_mean_by_rationality/.

cruelty in a passive demeanor. The indifference to factories exploding, sending soldiers off to murder civilians in wars, or to cars lacking safety standards and the company choosing to take the lawsuits because it's less of a financial loss are all forms of antiquated rationality. Any person or groups of people who conduct such acts aren't being rational; they are being misanthropic. Moreover, such acts cause people to distrust and seriously question an organization or person who would commit such horrific acts because it goes against our instincts of self-preservation and our empathy for the victims. In the long term, a business, nation-state, or peoples that would conduct such horrific behavior are condemned by the public, distrusted by other organizations that assumed they had a better grip on the situation, and they receive a permanent negative mark on history that continues to lead to antagonism or aversion from the peoples who were wronged and by people who have empathy for the victims. It coincides with the metaphorical term of shooting oneself in the foot.

As surprising as this may seem, empathy is fundamentally rational and all logical decision-making itself is grounded in emotion as part of human biology.[135] The assumption that rationality needs to be emotionless is both wrong and self-defeating.[136] It creates a coherent framework of needing to be evil to be wealthy and perniciously implies that human nature is innately predisposed to the concept of evil. The good and evil paradigm and the disproportionate focus of the national media on wrongful acts of the wealthy serve to justify this belief. Examples include news reports focusing upon politicians who have stolen taxpayer monies, focusing on celebrities who cheat the tax system, and focusing on the stupid actions undertaken by specific celebrities. Compare that disproportionate focus to news reports of billionaires who are alleviating world poverty, wealthy people who have given millions to charities for treatment of diseases harming children or cancer research, and essentially any other news report pertaining to positive actions by the

---

33. [135] Camp, Jim. "Decisions Are Emotional, Not Logical: the Neuroscience behind Decision Making." *Big Think*, Big Think, 11 June 2012, bigthink.com/experts-corner/decisions-are-emotional-not-logical-the-neuroscience-behind-decision-making.

34. [136] Galef, Julia. "The Straw Vulcan, Julia Galef Skepticon 4." *YouTube*, YouTube, 17 Aug. 2013, www.youtube.com/watch?v=Fv1nMc-k0N4.

wealthy.[137] Worse still, some wealthy people themselves may believe that acts of "evil" are justified to "get ahead" of others because of this self-destructive belief. Thus these people wrongfully commit themselves to grievous financial acts that weaken themselves and the confidence of their clients such as the economic recession of 2008 – 2009. Yet, the belief itself is what makes it a reality and it ultimately hurts the long-term confidence in capitalism. As recent charities by the wealthy have shown, this doesn't have to be true and it is an untenable position to generalize all wealthy people as evil and greedy.

Modern Politics and Antiquated Rationality

International relations often have the most brutal consequences upon the average citizens of all countries due to the actions of their political leaders. I would be remiss not to discuss the aspects of self-hatred and tribalism that is promoted by religious

---

35. [137] Boseley, Sarah. "How Bill and Melinda Gates helped save 122m lives – and what they want to solve next." *The Guardian*, Guardian News and Media, 14 Feb. 2017, www.theguardian.com/world/2017/feb/14/bill-gates-philanthropy-warren-buffett-vaccines-infant-mortality.

perceptions of events. The oldest and most impactful political theory

that is still used – amid varied forms – is the Realist Theory of

International Relations. While the theory's origins were from

Thucydides, the West has used this theory as the de facto guide to

international relations throughout the world and it has resulted in

sectarianism, the most brutal human rights crimes, and the weakening

of Western power.

The Realist Theory of International Relations posits that the

international order is anarchic; State's act "rational" for their self-

interest and try to maximize their power.[138] The only way to prevent

total destruction is usually either hegemony or a balance of power.[139]

Unfortunately, this conceptual framework leads to States fighting

among themselves and trying to weaken the power of other States

through acts of war, brutal oppression, genocide, counterfeit money,

36. [138] Viotti, Paul R., and Mark V. Kauppi. Chapter 2: Realism: The State,
    Power, and the Balance of Power (55-197). *International relations theory:
    realism, pluralism, globalism.* 3rd ed., Macmillan, 1998.

37. [139] Jentleson, Bruce W. *American foreign policy: the dynamics of choice in
    the 21st century.* 4th ed., Norton, 2010.

and promoting sectarianism. As a result, a pernicious and ubiquitous narrative to highlight the positive aspects of their own culture as morally good and all other civilizations as morally corrupt is the prominent narrative of all national news outlets in every civilization. When such a narrative cannot be easily constructed, then the news usually shifts to celebrity culture within the country. That is why there was a ubiquitous focus on Paris Hilton's sex tape when the US began its invasion of Iraq and bombed the homes of Iraqi civilians. This is also why the fictional narrative of humanitarian intervention is so persistent; better military equipment doesn't mean differentiating civilians from enemy soldiers or even children from adults – it just means being more effective at killing.[140] Attempts at obfuscating, demonizing, or minimizing the violence in wars reveals the ignorance and falsity of the good and evil paradigm; it is ignoring human violence conducted to a perceived out-group for the sake of cultural self-worship. As stated before, the good and evil ideology would

---

38. [140] Hedges, Chris. *War Is a Force That Gives Us Meaning*. PublicAffairs, 2002.

compel a country to view other peoples – and entire countries – as mostly evil and villainous to justify our nation's violence upon them.

World leaders and politicians would be compelled to harm peoples of other nations through sanctions, wars, covert operations, false flag operations, and to highlight demonizing them throughout the media because of the coherent belief of maximizing the nation-state's power by minimizing the power of other nation-states.[141] Yet, the minimizing of other nations results in spreading sectarianism within the foreign nation-state that ultimately threatens the safety of all other nation-states. When the US pulled out of Iraq in 2011, both the Democrat and Republican party proceeded to try to widen the sectarian differences in Iraq by supporting a Shia leader who closed off hospitals, educational facilities, jobs, and political participation for the Sunni population of Iraq. Due to the lack of actual knowledge behind why the invasion of Iraq happened, Sunni Iraqis likely felt desperate after a war that destroyed their homes, caused severe psychological damage to them and their children, and left them with a

---

39. [141] Jentleson, Bruce W. *American foreign policy: the dynamics of choice in the 21st century*. 4th ed., Norton, 2010.

government that shut them out from being able to live decent lives; this likely contributed in insurgency and terrorism spreading. After a couple years of protests resulting in nothing being changed, the peaceful protests changed to violent tactics, the terrorist Abu Bakr al-Baghdadi rose to power and further threatened the stability of the entire region by capitalizing on the suffering of the Sunnis by offering them money, food, housing, and a future once they ousted the corrupt Shia government from power. The US, being economically bound to the global economic interests of its closest allies in the Gulf, was forced to reenter into another war. But this third war in Iraq is the result of the Realist ideology of weakening other countries under the false assumption that it maximizes the stronger nation-state's power. The false axioms of the Realist theory, implicit in-group and out-group norms, and the religiously motivated belief in good and evil are to blame.

This isn't the first time that the West has conducted such behavior; the conflicts of Israel-Palestine, Pakistan-India, North and South Korea, and – more recently – the break-up of North and South

Sudan were formed by the Western powers spreading sectarianism by putting an extremist minority group in power to form policies that discriminated upon the masses and divided the people. Other ways the policy objective of the Realist theory is conducted is by creating separate public facilities and emphasizing the differences by favoring one of the groups over the others to sow discord that resulted in protests for equality, then shutting those protests down by colluding with a government that ignores their citizens protests and takes bribes from Western governments. Western governments have also aided autocratic governments in the torture and imprisonment of protestors. The results of these actions are prolonged wars in the Middle East in the case of Iraq, terrorism rising in the Middle East, the prolonged threat of terrorists gaining nuclear weapons in Pakistan, the exacerbated holy war between Israel and Palestine, and the prolonged enmity between various cultures that ultimately force the West into longer conflicts that weaken its own power. Historically, the realist theory of international relations played a focal factor in the Holocaust; the weakening of Germany by the allied powers intensified the hatred for the minority group, increased conspiracy theorists about Jewish people, and increased the religious differences that resulted in discrimination and then mass genocide. It resulted in another war after World War 1 that ultimately destroyed European hegemony over the world and engendered a Cold War that could have wiped out all human civilizations.

The Realist theory of international relations creates an anti-capitalist mindset that ultimately poses the worst threats to the longevity of capitalism. Imperialism is a personified version of the Realist theory and resulted in some of the most egregious human rights crimes throughout history.[142] Most of the countries that became communist did so because they conflated capitalism with the grotesque human rights crimes done to them by Europe. The message of Socialism, of a united civilization that doesn't fall into greed, was far more appealing to them at the time. Obviously, communism is a failure and led to despotic regimes that committed their own human

---

40. [142] Jentleson, Bruce W. *American foreign policy: the dynamics of choice in the 21st century.* 4th ed., Norton, 2010.

rights crimes. However, capitalism's lack of concern for workers in unsafe working conditions, child slavery, and legal indemnification when factories explode and kill people will only result in a resurgence of socialist sentiments. The realist theory and capitalist permissiveness of these egregious crimes only result in the weakening of economic power and distrust from the people. Worst of all, placing incompetent autocratic rulers in power, permitting human rights abuses, committing egregious human rights crimes such as bombing campaigns, and other horrors are expected to cause the slow downfall of a nation-state under the realist theory. The realist theory expects that the strongest nation-states will slowly erode in power.[143] These methods create a fatalistic view that all States must combat each other but eventually the strong States succumb to decline and become disempowered. Theorists foolishly treat this as a so-called inevitability of the anarchic system of States and States take actions purportedly for their so-called self-interest that result in their own

---

41. [143] Viotti, Paul R., and Mark V. Kauppi. Chapter 2: Realism: The State, Power, and the Balance of Power (55-197). *International relations theory: realism, pluralism, globalism.* 3rd ed., Macmillan, 1998.

slow self-destruction. In what way is this system either rational or positive for any nation-state? It leads to self-harm and treats such senseless actions as intelligent. It is the faultiness of religious axioms blended into cultural expectations about rationality that have created this self-defeating theory.

Modern rationality disagrees with the self-interest premise of antiquated rationality and points out its flaws; weakening other peoples will only give rise to sworn enemies, weakening others will drain your resources in dealing with the enemy, and you will have destroyed a potential ally that could have added to your strength.[144] This is true for employment, for friendship, and for nation-states. If a nation-state antagonizes you after aiding them then find a nation-state that is more suitable for your needs. Compare the European Union to jingoism that resulted in the two World Wars. Even in the worst economic recession thus far in history, the European Union is still a better option than the great depression that contributed to events

---

42. [144] Yudkowsky, Eliezer. "What Do We Mean By "Rationality"?" *Less Wrong*, 16 Mar. 2009, lesswrong.com/lw/31/what_do_we_mean_by_rationality/.

leading to the Holocaust and World War 2.[145] Mass poverty and

economic recession are still better social conditions than mass world

war. Empowerment is rational and disempowerment only leads to

weakening oneself and self-ruination.

43. [145] Roser, Max. "Visual History of The Rise of Political Freedom and the Decrease in Violence." *Visual History of The Rise of Political Freedom and the Decrease in Violence*. Web. 3 Jan. 2016.

Chapter 3: The Afterlife

This subject matter is probably the most difficult among the multitude of topics pertaining to religion and human life. I suspect that some, if not most, religious extremists probably fall into extremism because they want to believe that their loved ones are in the afterlife or other religious equivalents. This is probably the real reason why atheists are loathed in many countries; billboard signs and self-exalted demonstrations by atheists insulting religion seem hateful because it means that people will never see their deceased loved ones again. Those billboard signs are tacit and obnoxious arguments that those loved ones aren't happily living on in some form. I will try to be more sensitive and respectful in this section of the chapter; I wholeheartedly apologize if anything in this chapter offends anyone who has lost a loved one and has turned to religion for guidance on the matter.

A significant amount of people who have faith probably don't believe in a higher power for the explicit purpose of worshipping a

God or Gods; people believe in their faith because they want their deceased friends or relatives to be happy and to see them again in the future. A belief in deities seems endemically tied to such a viewpoint. What could an atheist viewpoint offer to someone who has faith because they have lost a child? Logical arguments wouldn't matter and there is absolutely nothing that an atheist viewpoint could offer to lessen the emotional pain. For those who have lost loved ones, the best response that I can offer is that what you're actually having faith in is for your loved ones lives to have meaning; along with the obvious desire to see them again. In that case, believing in a deity is just a tool for the sake of celebrating your loved ones in your memories. Please consider this: *your loved ones are the real gods that you worship*. In the context of Christianity and Islam, when people make statements such as "your loved one is smiling down from heaven" what you're really doing is deifying your loved ones in your own mind. Systems of theology are used as tools to worship the people that you have lost. This is not a radical concept. Within ancient theology, such as Roman Polytheism, human beings themselves were deified as gods. Within early Christianity, people became lauded as saints for their positive deeds for the people, which is simply another form of deification without the supposedly arrogant implication of a human revered as a God. Deification, sainthood, Mahatma, and other honorifics are attempts to praise and honor our loved ones as Gods themselves. It is for the hope that they're remembered for all eternity. Removing faith takes away the immortalization of the dead and that immortalization is itself a reflection of people's feelings for their loved ones.

What should the answer be? Should people simply identify such beliefs as falsehoods? Should atheists condemn grieving people who strongly believe because they lost a loved one? No, absolutely not. In the context of people who have lost children, there is really nothing that atheism could offer to assuage their inner grief and the best answer I could possibly say is that I'm sorry for your loss. However, I would say their lives have intrinsic meaning because of how much those who have lost them choose to devote their lives to worshipping and, in that sense, deifying them. In regards to deceased people who've lived full lives, I would argue that much of their life has helped the work of others: children who grow more successful than their parents usually have their parents to thank for their support, love, and dedication. In other cases, philosophers who have formed philosophical arguments usually have their views adapted and built upon by admirers who form their own, scientific studies build upon or refute the previous works of past scientists, and the same can be applied to technology, laws, and virtually any form of human progress.[146] People can choose to celebrate their loved ones by running charity drives in the name of their loved ones for positive causes. Unfortunately, there are negative aspects of human progress that shouldn't be ignored, such as the methods of killing in warfare. In the end, it is due to what and how we as a species choose to improve about our existence. I would argue that all of the non-violent forms of progress do have intrinsic meaning. To the people of the 1700s and further back, we would be viewed as Gods with what we can do in our

---

1. [146] Nietzsche, Friedrich Wilhelm. "Chapter XXXIV: Self-Surpassing (108-111)" *Thus spake Zarathustra: a book for all and none*. Translated by Thomas Common, PDF ed., T. Common, 1908.

everyday lives. Even something like a cell phone may have brought cries of shock and claims of witchcraft because it would seem bizarre.

Death Worship

Religion is a worship of death. It wouldn't be inaccurate to say that religion is simply the term for popularized death cults. Terms such as afterlife, heaven, and nirvana are simply positive attributions to what is essentially valuing an imaginary world where the dead reside.[147][148] Heaven and hell are contradistinctions that serve the convenience of people; everyone favorable is in heaven and everyone despised is in hell. Consequently, heaven and nirvana are depictions of worshipping a *blessed death*; that is, a death for good people where they live on happily. Hell is the opposite; a death for evil people who suffer for the crimes they have caused upon humanity. Therefore, religion is sanctified death worship.

---

2. [147] Nietzsche, Friedrich Wilhelm. *THE ANTICHRIST*. Translated by H. L. Mencken, The Project Gutenberg, 2006.

3. [148]Nietzsche, Friedrich Wilhelm. "Chapter IX: Preachers of Death (50-52)" *Thus spake Zarathustra: a book for all and none*. Translated by Thomas Common, PDF ed., T. Common, 1908.

From the self-negation of asceticism and good/evil thinking, humans have largely concocted this fantasy for their own convenience. Instead of trying to find and apprehend war criminals, people are more prone to becoming apathetic to human rights crimes of war criminals. It is precisely the belief that war criminals are going to hell and good people are being sent to heaven that causes the pervasive apathy. A war criminal that has slaughtered hundreds of thousands and then lives a wholesome life before dying a natural death is argued to be in hell suffering for their sins and the innocent people that the war criminal killed are argued to be in heaven. It is a fantasy that only serves to feed our desire for revenge upon the war criminal and our desire to believe in a just world for the victims; it is a convenience that religious believers have construed to satisfy themselves instead of accepting the true horrors of wrongdoings.[149] The impotence towards fighting against human rights crimes, the convenience of fanciful thinking, and the belief in good and evil

---

4. [149] Nietzsche, Friedrich Wilhelm. *On the genealogy of morals: a polemical tract.* Translated by Ian Johnston, PDF, Richer Resources Publications, 2014.

regarding what happens after death create a disdainful level of apathy towards all crimes against humanity. The religious attempt at an easy answer and anchoring towards the importance of souls creates a permissive indifference towards deplorable acts of savagery that is promoted through in-group and out-group differences of racial background, culture, religion, and national identity.

In general, the concept of a soul is a psychotic and narcissistic belief to hold. While seemingly innocuous and treated as normal within most communities across the world, the belief in the soul leads to pernicious consequences. The belief in a soul encourages people to view life itself as a test and to see suffering from diseases, poverty, and other forms of suffering as deep and meaningful for the purpose of an afterlife instead of taking on our personal challenges to work towards making a better future in our real life. Worse still, the belief in a soul inculcates us into antipathy towards life, to see everything as a nauseating struggle that is too difficult to understand or meaningfully contend with, and fosters a binary good versus evil worldview in which everything that has power is automatically assumed to be evil and the powerless are always viewed as good and righteous. The chief problem with the belief in a soul is that it is unhealthy for our physical wellbeing.[150][151] It is an unfounded belief that posits we will have all of our thinking and speech faculties in a deceased form of ourselves after our own deaths. Instead of critically examining the various maladies that afflict us as we age like Alzheimer's disease, potential physical injuries that require amputations of body parts, and personality changes due to dementia or drugs needed to keep ourselves alive; people who believe in souls see it all as an abstract form of decay in preparation for death where all those physical afflictions won't matter. The belief in the existence of a soul is a narcissistic belief in personal immortality outside of the physical body[152] and it is psychotic because of a rabid anti-materialist perspective that is inculcated on seeing our physical suffering as

---

5.   [150] Nietzsche, Friedrich Wilhelm. *On the genealogy of morals: a polemical tract*. Translated by Ian Johnston, PDF, Richer Resources Publications, 2014.

6.   [151] Nietzsche, Friedrich Wilhelm. *Thus spake Zarathustra: a book for all and none*. Translated by Thomas Common, PDF ed., T. Common, 1908.

7.   [152] Nietzsche, Friedrich Wilhelm. Aphorism 43. *THE ANTICHRIST*. Translated by H. L. Mencken, The Project Gutenberg, 2006.

either morally good or necessary in preparation for the afterlife where our immortal self will go.[153] Dealing with death is tragic and painful, but the focus on an illusionary immortal self and anti-materialism can lead to devastating consequences. Despite nuanced philosophical conceptions, anti-materialism in more simplified religious conceptual frameworks can lead to disastrous and ridiculous activities such as anti-vaccination movements that harm entire communities and lead to the death of children as a result of a few handful of evocative stories of individual cases reacting poorly to vaccines due to unique health circumstances that aren't reflective of the average population. These anecdotes are often guiding some people's judgment instead of statistical trends on large populations to get a fuller picture of health issues. In short, using anecdotes to tell a good versus evil story that conflate qualified medical professionals like doctors and nurses with supposed evil managers in companies that mass-produce drugs.[154] No distinction is made on either the medical professionals and the drug

---

8.   [153] Nietzsche, Friedrich Wilhelm. *THE ANTICHRIST*. Translated by H. L. Mencken, The Project Gutenberg, 2006.
9.   [154] Ispas, Alexa. *Psychology and politics: a social identity perspective*. Psychology Press, 2014.

companies; nor is any distinction made between drug companies that may be doing positive work for the majority of people compared to ones that have been accused of scandals. Instead of researching issues for a clearer understanding of problems, there is simply anti-intellectual contempt and distrust based on an affect heuristic on anecdotal examples. A story of a child having a bad reaction can certainly be heartbreaking to read or watch and people getting a plethora of anecdotes across different countries from online can lead to fear of vaccines.[155][156] However, it is in ignorance of statistical averages and fails to account for the hundreds of millions who don't have any unique health defects that cause such reactions and live healthier lives with less worry about diseases that could harm their bodily health.

The anti-materialist mindset towards medical health can lead to using homeopathy cures such as from Christian Science culture,

---

10. [155] Kahneman, Daniel. Chapter 8: How Judgments Happen (89-96) *Thinking, fast and slow*. Farrar, Straus and Giroux, 2015.

11. [156] Kahneman, Daniel. Chapter 30: Rare Events (322-333) *Thinking, fast and slow*. Farrar, Straus and Giroux, 2015.

nonsensical pseudoscience like horoscope readings and crystal

healing, and folk homeopathy carried over from family traditions

centered around other types of superstitious thinking. Often these

pseudo-scientific beliefs ignore legitimate medical treatment based on

qualified medical professionals for special pleading arguments about

certain symbols like the Cross harboring divine qualities, beliefs

about holy water, and beliefs centered around casting out demons

from people who are physically sick. The main focus of all these

pernicious beliefs is that they are about healing the soul under the

wrong belief that the soul actually exists and takes precedent over the

physical body.[157] There is no evidence for the existence of a soul in

science. While consciousness isn't fully understood as of this writing,

conditions brought upon by dementia and Alzheimer disease are

evidence that the existence of an immortal self that people refer to as

a soul lacks credibility.

Even when ostensibly presenting themselves as creating

hospitals to heal people, people with strong religious faith may

---

12. [157] Nietzsche, Friedrich Wilhelm. *Thus spake Zarathustra: a book for all and none*. Translated by Thomas Common, PDF ed., T. Common, 1908.

instead create poor houses that do little more than take pleasure in the suffering of others to serve as their own emotional connection to the God they worship as was the case with Mother Teresa.[158] One may question why a religious believer would do such a horrible activity and praise themselves for it. It is because poverty, sickness, and suffering aren't seen as issues to take actionable steps against in order to make the lives of a community healthier, but instead as something to revere as sacred, proof of a simple truth that death exists for all people regardless of their economic status, and it is presented as something profound beyond the human experience. It is a worship of death prompted by the belief in a human soul.[159][160] It is allowing the physical suffering of others in order to feel a narcissistic pleasure in the belief in one's own delusion of immortality. This type of fanciful thinking can also lead to antipathy towards hierarchies based on

13. [158] Hitchens, Christopher. "Christopher Hitchens: Hell's Angel: Mother Teresa (English Subtitles)." *YouTube*, BBC News, 7 Jan. 2015, youtu.be/NK7l_IhtKNU.

14. [159] Nietzsche, Friedrich Wilhelm. Aphorism 43. *THE ANTICHRIST*. Translated by H. L. Mencken, The Project Gutenberg, 2006.

15. [160] Nietzsche, Friedrich Wilhelm. *Thus spake Zarathustra: a book for all and none*. Translated by Thomas Common, PDF ed., T. Common, 1908.

expertise in fields that provide meaningful work that help millions of people everyday like economics, agriculture, waterways, railroads, aviation, healthcare, energy plants, businesses, banks, and government to instead give a blanket view that everything that has power is corrupt and to offer a form of equality that isn't equality at all.[161] Depending upon the particular religion, they can be hierarchies based on ancient stories that celebrate end of the world prophecies that indoctrinate people to give their discretionary income, one morning of every week of their time, and control of their sex lives to the religious leader of a congregation or the local mosque which often discriminate against women and LGBT people. In other religious groups, there are beliefs about reincarnation that create widespread societal friction on the basis of reincarnating into the top of the hierarchy in another life or going beyond reincarnation. Regardless of the specifics, religion offers hierarchies of insanity based upon devotion to ancient stories while vilifying expertise based upon hard

---

16. [161] Nietzsche, Friedrich Wilhelm. *THE ANTICHRIST*. Translated by H. L. Mencken, The Project Gutenberg, 2006.

work, lifelong experience, and rigorous academic learning.[162] Of course, there are deeply religious people that are part of hospitals, schools, and so forth who make positive contributions to society, but that is a non-sequitur in terms of proving their beliefs to be true. For comparison, many terrorist organizations like Hezbollah and Hamas do charity work in their local communities, do their charity drives validate their Islamist ideals to be the truth about reality? Selflessly helping others doesn't prove that a person's religion is true.

The most overt form of death worship is dying for the faith. While celebrating self-sacrifice may seem morally good and the noblest form of heroism that a person can do for their religion, it is ultimately celebrating someone who chose to die upholding the rules and traditions of a religious faith. A religion provides moral guidelines to regulate behavior and honors people who regulate themselves more than others because it shows a deeper conviction to the religious faith. The celebration of self-renunciation within religion eventually devolves into a celebration of death for the honor of the

---

17. [162] Nietzsche, Friedrich Wilhelm. *THE ANTICHRIST*. Translated by H. L. Mencken, The Project Gutenberg, 2006.

particular religion. The death of people who are killed for upholding their conviction to their religious faith is celebrated as proof of the faith's intrinsic goodness and proof of its truth. This is a pathological argument that perceives institutionalized insanity as an act of moral goodness. It is an explicit call upon people to die for their faith and is therefore indisputably an explicit worship of death. *To put it simply: dying for your religious faith doesn't prove your religion is true.*[163] *Thus, dying for your religious beliefs doesn't mean anything. It doesn't matter how strong you feel your convictions towards your religious faith are or how strongly someone you may know believed and died for them.* People would have difficulty to find any other system that asks them to die for the sake of proving the system is both morally good and to showcase its validity. To give more consideration to this criticism, consider this question proposed by Friedrich Nietzsche when he tackled this subject: Is there truly any meaningful difference between having conviction for your religious beliefs and

---

18. [163] Nietzsche, Friedrich Wilhelm. Aphorism 53. *THE ANTICHRIST.* Translated by H. L. Mencken, The Project Gutenberg, 2006.

believing in a lie?[164] To further add to this point, consider his challenging question with two questions added on: *What is the difference between having a strong conviction to your faith-based claim and believing in a lie? For someone else who believes in another religion, what is the difference between them believing in their faith-based claim and a lie? Why do you see your faith-based claim as fundamentally different from that other person's faith-based claim?*

Dying for the faith loses the pathological admiration that religious believers confer to the ideology when comparisons are made between different religious faiths. If self-sacrifice in the name of Judaism is the truth, then what use is any religiously motivated sacrifice in the name of Jesus Christ? Conversely, if Christianity is the truth then what is the value of any sacrifice in the name of Judaism? This pathological framework would instill people to sacrifice themselves so that the dead people on their side would validate their

---

19. [164] Nietzsche, Friedrich Wilhelm. Aphorism 55. *THE ANTICHRIST.* Translated by H. L. Mencken, The Project Gutenberg, 2006.

religious faith as the ultimate truth; what else can we call religious wars but just that kind of process? The self-destructive process continues through a pernicious circular reasoning that creates a sunk-cost fallacy.[165] Religious people celebrate the purportedly noble self-sacrifices to encourage more people to sacrifice themselves for the religion. In brief, circular reasoning is the logical fallacy of placing the premise of an argument into its conclusion in order to argue the conclusion is true[166] and the example in this critique is the following: Because people die for a holy book then the holy book is true because people selflessly chose to die for the holy book. Thus, in a horrific form of circular reasoning and the sunk-cost fallacy: to validate the past sacrifices as divine truth of the religion itself, the religion celebrates past sacrifices to make people favorably predisposed to sacrificing themselves in the present to continue this in-group self-exaltation as a means of arguing in favor of the so-called truth of a

---

20. [165] Kahneman, Daniel. Chapter 31: Risk Policies (334-341) and Keeping Score (342 - 352) *Thinking, fast and slow*. Farrar, Straus and Giroux, 2015.

21. [166] "Circular Reasoning." *Https://Www.logicallyfallacious.com*, www.logicallyfallacious.com/tools/lp/Bo/LogicalFallacies/66/Circular-Reasoning.

religious faith. This creates a historic celebration of human sacrifice as the noblest and purest act of religious faith. It is a sanctified call to death for all religious believers specifically to celebrate the religious faith. This is a powerful force within religion that shouldn't be ignored because it displays how deranged religion truly is.

Suicide Worship

Martyrdom exists in all religious faiths; despite the anecdotal popularization of Islam being a religion of suicide bombers, it has existed in both militant Christianity through the human sacrifice bombers – or proxy bombers as the news media called them – in Northern Ireland.[167] They would place bombs in the packages carried by kidnapped civilians and detonate them when the civilians were forced into delivering the packages by gunpoint or by having a bomb forcibly strapped onto them.[168] Militant Hinduism assisted in

---

22. [167] POGATCHNIK, SHAWN. "IRA Proxy Bombings Kill 6 Troops, Civilian : Northern Ireland: The attack by the terrorist group is the deadliest against British forces in two years." *Los Angeles Times*, Los Angeles Times, 25 Oct. 1990, articles.latimes.com/1990-10-25/news/mn-4248_1_northern-ireland.

23. [168] McCann, Eamonn. "Real IRA's lust for violence matters more than

conducting suicide bombings in Sri Lanka against the discrimination

and genocide of the ruling Buddhists. In all cases, all forms of

suicidal terror were predominately motivated by overthrowing a

perceived tyrannical ruler. In the case of the Tamil Tiger militia that

was mostly comprised of Hindus, it was against brutal Buddhist

oppression.[169] In the case of Northern Ireland, it was to gain

independence from British rule since the British had a history of

human rights crimes and genocide. In the case of suicidal terror in the

Middle East, it is to overthrow the military presence of the United

States so that the people of the Middle East can overthrow the Islamic

dictators that commit egregious human rights crimes upon their own

people while giving favorable economic benefits to the rest of the

world. While suicidal terrorism doesn't originate from any particular

---

ideology on the streets | Eamonn McCann." *The Guardian*, Guardian News and Media, 21 Aug. 2010, www.theguardian.com/uk/2010/aug/22/northern-ireland-dissidents-peace-process.

24. [169] Eggen, Dan, and Scott Wilson. "Suicide Bombs Potent Tools of Terrorists." *The Washington Post*, WP Company, 17 July 2005, www.washingtonpost.com/archive/politics/2005/07/17/suicide-bombs-potent-tools-of-terrorists/e11ed483-9936-45c0-b6c6-2653d4519ff5/?utm_term=.c23458392a4a.

religious faith, it seems to be the theological and intellectual conclusion of the doctrine of noble self-sacrifice that exists in all religious faiths. In the case of military tactics, it would mean sacrificing one unit to bring colossal damage to the enemy and it can have religious defense through the notion of sacrificing oneself for a divine purpose of fighting against evil. The use of "good against evil" to self-exalt the suicide bombers' group as morally good to fight against evil tyranny could be included as a reasoning behind suicidal terrorism. The belief of good versus evil and the doctrine of noble self-sacrifice would be the culprits when intermingled with suicidal depression of the person who blows themselves up.

Please consider this, isn't it the doctrine of noble self-sacrifice that feeds the narcissistic impulse of being a hero for a greater purpose? Moreover, this doctrine is a self-worship of one's own death as the greatest event for a divine purpose. Behind this supposedly noble ideology is a morbid self-hate and desire for suicide.[170][171] In

---

25. [170] Lester, David. "Female Suicide Bombers: Clues from Journalists." *Suicidology Online*, Suicidology Online, 14 Nov. 2011, www.suicidology-online.com/pdf/SOL-2011-2-62-66.pdf.

regards to suicide bombings and religious wars, it is entirely possible that a paradoxical belief in self-hate and an exaggerated sense of self-importance when using weapons is what motivates the ideology of noble self-sacrifice. Their desire for suicide and self-importance intermingle to form an utterly depraved belief that celebrates their own suicide as a magnificent event against an enemy that is viewed as an abstract form of tyranny. It is precisely for that reason that suicidal terrorism is deliberate suicide in retaliation towards tyrannical domestic government or foreign governments perceived as aggressors, the suicidal bomber would feel a sense of pleasure at lashing out at foreign aggressors by making their own death be personally perceived as higher in importance in service to a political ideology. In conflation with the political context, the good and evil dynamic along with the religious belief in self-renunciation from asceticism would celebrate the belief in self-sacrifice as a divine service for a higher purpose. Similar to oppressed groups who lash

26. [171] Lankford, Adam. "Martyr myth: Inside the minds of suicide bombers." *New Scientist*, 3 July 2013, www.newscientist.com/article/mg21929240-200-martyr-myth-inside-the-minds-of-suicide-bombers/.

out in violence against those who make them powerless, the suicide bomber could perceive their suicide as the only way to improve their sense of significance and may feel empowered by perceiving themselves as above their aggressors through personal self-sacrifice with the pleasure of knowing they'll never have to deal with life's hardships, they'll never have to suffer their feelings of hopelessness, or live through systems of oppressive cruelty ever again.[172] Their self-sacrifice would be perceived and celebrated as a leap of faith, a poignant moment of self-sacrifice (according to political groups whose interests of fighting a stronger army through the sacrifice of one soldier has been served and distraught family members of the deceased who try to find any positive in their mourning), and as rising above their "evil" oppressor.[173] Political groups that the suicidal terrorist is a part of would further reinforce this by celebrating the

27. [172] Lankford, Adam. "Exposing false 'martyrs' as suicidal." *The Jerusalem Post | JPost.Com*, 17 Feb. 2013, www.jpost.com/Opinion/Op-Ed-Contributors/Exposing-false-martyrs-as-suicidal.

28. [173] Lankford, Adam. "Exposing false 'martyrs' as suicidal." *The Jerusalem Post | JPost.Com*, 17 Feb. 2013, www.jpost.com/Opinion/Op-Ed-Contributors/Exposing-false-martyrs-as-suicidal.

death as a form of self-sacrifice and awarding the family of the

suicidal individual with stable living conditions, the significance of

which shouldn't be understated; the suicidal terrorist will finally be

proving themselves capable and could feel secure in the knowledge

they helped their family by giving their lives to what they're

inculcated to believe is a greater cause.[174] Martyrdom and self-

sacrifice are merely semantic terms for sanctifying suicide, the only

difference is that a political objective is attached to suicide to make a

suicide bomber feel their life is finally above their oppressor through

suicidal retaliation that has trite terminology to extol the perception

that it's somehow blessed.[175]

Arguably, this ideology of noble self-sacrifice could apply to

soldiers in war. It is possible that applies to some people within some

countries, but nationalistic fervor is just as much of a reason for

---

29. [174] McDermott, Rose. Chapter 5: Behavior (119-152). *Political Psychology in International Relations*. Ann Arbor: U of Michigan, 2004. Print.

30. [175] Lankford, Adam. "What You Don't Understand about Suicide Attacks." *Scientific American*, 27 July 2015, www.scientificamerican.com/article/what-you-don-t-understand-about-suicide-attacks/.

warfare and there have been atheists who have went to war

throughout human history. Even so, there is a difference between

sacrificing oneself to be in heaven as opposed to maintaining

government power, sovereignty, and the welfare of a civilian

populace. It depends upon the individual soldier, but there can be

overlap and shallow differences within these conceptual frameworks.

However, it doesn't discount the actions of soldiers who serve for the

convenience of the public. Governments across the world should do

more to provide better treatment for their soldiers; from hospital care,

to education, to treatment for understandable psychological issues

suffered from prolonged exposure to war, and to payments that they

deserve. For example, it is rather dismaying to observe the problems

with soldiers getting paid in a timely fashion in the US.[176][177][178]

31. [176] Carr, Kelly, and Scot J. Paltrow. "Reuters Investigates - UNACCOUNTABLE: The Pentagon's bad bookkeeping." *Reuters*, Thomson Reuters, 2 July 2013, www.reuters.com/investigates/pentagon/#article/part1.

32. [177] Carr, Kelly, and Scot J. Paltrow. "Reuters Investigates - UNACCOUNTABLE: The Pentagon's bad bookkeeping." *Reuters*, Thomson Reuters, 2 July 2013, www.reuters.com/investigates/pentagon/#article/part2.

Another important point that should be noted is that while suicidal

terror does foster fear, hostility, and resentment; it can also bring

about resilience and stronger support for peace talks in opposition to

the aims of terrorist groups to spark fear and in some cases, to foster

further retaliation.[179][180]

The Eternal Death

Religion has routinely given positive characteristics to death.

In order to stymie the fear of the unknown and to make sense of it,

anthropomorphic and anthropocentric qualities were given to the

reality of death to make it more familiar and relatable to human

society and the individual's personal desires so that people felt a

---

33. [178] Carr, Kelly, and Scot J. Paltrow. "Reuters Investigates - UNACCOUNTABLE: The Pentagon's bad bookkeeping." *Reuters*, Thomson Reuters, 2 July 2013, www.reuters.com/investigates/pentagon/#article/part3.
34. [179] Lowe, Josh. "How Britain's history with the IRA made it resilient to attacks." *Newsweek*, 29 Mar. 2017, www.newsweek.com/london-attack-ira-terror-threat-severe-bomb-terrorism-573629.
35. [180] POGATCHNIK, SHAWN. "IRA Proxy Bombings Kill 6 Troops, Civilian : Northern Ireland: The attack by the terrorist group is the deadliest against British forces in two years." *Los Angeles Times*, Los Angeles Times, 25 Oct. 1990, articles.latimes.com/1990-10-25/news/mn-4248_1_northern-ireland.

comforting acquiescence with death and the pain of losing loved ones.

The concepts of the afterlife were reactionary concepts to the mass

death brought by diseases, war, famine, and the nihilism that these

horrors caused. The ancient world used rash judgments to find

meaning in their lives; diseases, wars, famine, and natural disasters

were seen as God's judgment.[181] Ancient people presumed that

stricter social conditions upon their communities, sacrificial rituals,

and coming of age rituals would bring good fortune to the community

to lessen those circumstances. As a result, death was sanitized and

given positive qualities to create a coherent framework that made

people believe they could escape their nihilistic feelings about the

world.[182]

Death changed from being understood as the end of life to

becoming part of some imaginary eternity. The imperfections of the

36. [181] Kahneman, Daniel. *Thinking, fast and slow*. Farrar, Straus and Giroux, 2015.

37. [182] Nietzsche, Friedrich Wilhelm. *On the genealogy of morals: a polemical tract*. Translated by Ian Johnston, PDF, Richer Resources Publications, 2014.

world no longer mattered because people would be sent to a "perfect world" after death.[183] All of the problems of the real world didn't matter anymore; people just had to go through the monotony and suffering as if it were a type of nausea so they could enter their perfect world as a reward.[184] Our wants, our feelings, and our decisions became "illusionary" because they were impermanent; they were redefined as part of a grander scheme for an eternal and perfect system that served humanity's convenience for wanting to feel safe from disease, wars, famines, and other horrors. The eternal world, Samsara unto moksha i.e. reincarnation unto self-liberation, the afterlife, and purgatory were what each ancient civilization wanted their world to be so that their suffering was meaningful. Humanity gave death a set of positive human characteristics to make death more

---

38. [183] Nietzsche, Friedrich Wilhelm. *THE ANTICHRIST*. Translated by H. L. Mencken, The Project Gutenberg, 2006.

39. [184] Nietzsche, Friedrich Wilhelm. *On the genealogy of morals: a polemical tract*. Translated by Ian Johnston, PDF, Richer Resources Publications, 2014.

relatable and comfortable to process as an event.[185][186] The humanizing of death and the convenience of there being a life after death can be seen in modern culture; from films depicting the so-called afterlife, to books that make death similar to the real world through the idea of talking inhabitants in a "world" that people can interact within, and iconography depicting beautiful deities, angels, and a perfect world as a reward for people who have strong faith.[187][188] The religious argument that people can "never know" what happens after death is an argument from ignorance that originates from our desire for a meaningful and everlasting life – the same desires that the ancient world had. But do you see the problem? People who pose that

40. [185] Webb, David. "Fritz Heider & Marianne Simmel: An Experimental Study of Apparent Behavior." *Psychology*, www.all-about-psychology.com/fritz-heider.html.

41. [186] Nietzsche, Friedrich Wilhelm. *On the genealogy of morals: a polemical tract*. Translated by Ian Johnston, PDF, Richer Resources Publications, 2014.

42. [187] Webb, David. "Fritz Heider & Marianne Simmel: An Experimental Study of Apparent Behavior." *Psychology*, www.all-about-psychology.com/fritz-heider.html.

43. [188] Kahneman, Daniel. *Thinking, fast and slow*. Farrar, Straus and Giroux, 2015.

argument are attempting to equalize the fact of death with fictional desires for a perfect world. It is explicitly to make the believer feel better about their inevitable death and the horrors of the world. The iconography and beliefs of the afterlife, reincarnation, and other ideas about eternal death aren't necessarily self-centered beliefs either. While the ultimate goal may be to feel more comfortable with death; the reasons for believing in the afterlife is also because of humanity's desire for a just world for victims that they'll never know. The imaginary eternal world can be considered a just world fallacy out of empathy for innocent victims throughout the real world.[189] It was a rash answer to a deeply complex problem that can't be solved easily.

The concept of God was probably a primitive attempt at creating familiar and humanistic characteristics upon the morbid feelings when observing death.[190] An eternal, perfect, and loving

44. [189] Grinnell, Renée. "Just-World Hypothesis." *Encyclopedia of Psychology*, 17 July 2016, psychcentral.com/encyclopedia/just-world-hypothesis/.

45. [190] Webb, David. "Fritz Heider & Marianne Simmel: An Experimental Study of Apparent Behavior." *Psychology*, www.all-about-psychology.com/fritz-heider.html.

creator who had a plan beyond what the scope of our insignificance could comprehend was a more comforting and likable thought than the natural end of a life with no discernible way to understand diseases, natural disasters, and violence from neighboring tribes that attacked. It was a meaning formed through pattern recognition and rash judgments in order to understand the processes of the natural world that caused suffering.

Chapter 4: Open Interpretation and Coherent Religious Structures

The majority of religious believers use open interpretation in their understanding of their respective religion. This has led to a myriad of religious notions that usually try to stay neutral to the gap between religion and science. The God of the gaps, notions that changing personal opinions on social issues interpreted as people becoming closer to God (such as the issue of gay rights and more recently Transgender Rights for the Abrahamic faiths), and the rejection of untenable aspects of religious books such as the book of Leviticus in the Bible were concessions of religious beliefs to modernity. Stories about Adam and Eve in the Garden of Eden and Manu, the first man in Hinduism, are regarded as metaphorical instead of the divine truth originating from a higher power.

These concessions show a lack of awareness towards religious history; countless millions believed in the absolute truth of religious fables before science and modernity slowly destroyed the ability to justify those beliefs. The concept of science versus religion is a false argument because it doesn't delve into the true depth of the contentious issue. Science was never at war with religion; the 1800s were slowly weakening religion before Darwin's Origin of the species became popularized. *Religion has always been at war with modernity.* It doesn't matter how many born-again Christians can have the cognitive dissonance to believe in both science and religion; science will always seem at war with religion because science enhances modernity for the convenience of the public. Religion has a few generational successes through its cultural recidivism but such recidivism slowly erodes to social changes after each generation. Social media has made it easier to erode religious influence; it is easier to learn more about the world than ever before and people can fact-check anything they want. As a result, religious ideas will always be challenged by exposure to different peoples, cultures, ideologies, and lifestyles. Religion has been struggling against science, capitalism, women's liberation, sexual liberation, homosexual and transgender rights, freedom of speech, and the freedom of self-expression through art for centuries; the internet may allow mass ignorance to fester but it also allows challenges to beliefs from the interaction of opposing viewpoints.

The concept of open interpretation – the ability to pick and choose parables to follow and ignore the rest of the teachings of a religion – has allowed religion to remain compatible with modernity but eventually it'll no longer be possible. *Open interpretation ultimately reduces moral questions to personal preference.* For all of the refutations from the pious about the lack of positive moral teachings without religion, open interpretation has already rendered religious teachings to be ineffectual and obsolete. Arguably, modernity has supplanted religion and we are pretending otherwise to satisfy our own convenience because human societies are still unable to deal with a lack of objective meaning in life.

Open Interpretation and True Interpretation

When a religiously motivated atrocity occurs, people of the same religious faith as the attackers often contend that such barbaric actions are not the true interpretations of the religious faith. Whether it is Islamic terrorism, Christian militias slaughtering civilians in third world countries like the Central African Republic, shootings with explicitly religious call to arms, Buddhist beheadings in Myanmar, or the religious war for the so-called holy land by Jews, Christians, and Muslims for centuries unto our contemporary time; the majority of believers of a particular religious faith will always argue that such actions aren't true interpretations of their religious faith. This argument presents a total self-contradiction: if there are true interpretations of the faith then how can religion be openly interpretative? If religion *is* openly interpretative then how can the extremist interpretation of any religious faith be less valid than a moderate interpretation of the faith? Open interpretation would require both interpretations to be equally valid. If religion has a true interpretation, then which religious denomination of which specific religion is it? Despite my disagreements with them, New Atheists were correct in pointing out that the majority of believers in the Christian and Islamic religious denominations should expect to be in hell by a measure of probability should any specific denomination be proven true.

The issues with open interpretation exist because it is a set of logical fallacies; first, there is an appeal to purity. People disagree with or ignore the actions of other people within their religious affiliation to defend the innate goodness of the religious faith. Instead of taking into account the real life horrors that religion has caused, people argue that the horrible atrocities aren't a "true interpretation" or they argue that such actions aren't a reflection of God to defend their particular religious faith.[191] As a result, the apologists defending their faith ignore the human rights atrocities as an afterthought; the belief in God's mysterious plan can conveniently help any specific religious group ignore the victims who have died as a result of an

---

1. [191] Kahneman, Daniel. Chapter 9: Answering an Easier Question (97-104). *Thinking, fast and slow*. Farrar, Straus and Giroux, 2015.

interpretation of their religious faith.[192][193] The conviction to their faith expresses a depth of apathy and misanthropy towards the rest of the human species; the lives of perceived out-groups, who are the victims, are ignored just because they have no allegiance to the religious faith of the apologists.[194] The apologists have chosen the importance of their religious faith and their God over the purportedly less important affairs of human life.[195]

An example of a type of this defense occurred during the New York Public Library debate between Al Sharpton and Christopher Hitchens over the question of God. Sharpton questioned what Hitchens criticisms regarding heinous stories from the Bible, what the actions of religious extremists in the Middle East – using Christian, Muslim, and Jewish examples of Iraq and the so-called Holy Land,

2. [192] Kahneman, Daniel. *Thinking, fast and slow*. Farrar, Straus and Giroux, 2015.

3. [193] Cialdini, Robert B. Chapter 6: Authority (178-200). *Influence: Science and practice*. 4th ed., 21st Century Bks, 2002.

4. [194] Ispas, Alexa. *Psychology and politics: a social identity perspective*. Psychology Press, 2014.

5. [195] Cialdini, Robert B. Chapter 6: Authority (178-200). *Influence: Science and practice*. 4th ed., 21st Century Bks, 2002.

and other examples of religious atrocities had to do with the question of God and the moral order of the universe.[196] While Hitchens didn't have a direct response, it seemed like a particularly cruel attempt at ignoring the atrocities and violent teachings. It is a tacit admittance that faith in God is valued more highly than the lives of people who are killed by religion; Sharpton continued to use the universe as an example of why there needs to be moral order so that there are limits to what is permissible. Thus, God is removed or constantly redefined to suit the convenience of the believers while ignoring the atrocities that a belief in God has caused.[197] But consider this; if this were any other social system such as imperialism, communism, monarchies, or fascism then would we be questioning what these social systems had to do with the senseless human slaughter? Why should it not reflect negatively upon religion when the religious apologists are more likely to dismiss egregious human rights crimes as an afterthought? Most

---

6. [196] "Christopher Hitchens Debates Al Sharpton - New York Public." *YouTube*, YouTube, 6 Dec. 2011, www.youtube.com/watch?v=HPYxA8dYLBY.

7. [197] Kahneman, Daniel. *Thinking, fast and slow*. Farrar, Straus and Giroux, 2015.

importantly, what does the almost ubiquitous apathy by every religious majority towards human rights crimes in the name of their faith reveal about religious morality itself?

A second logical fallacy with open interpretation is the "moving the goalposts" fallacy. It can work concurrently with appeal to purity. Essentially, the parameters and axioms of the religious faith are constantly changed to defend the supposed innate goodness of the religion.[198] Open interpretations allows this shift to happen so that no argument can change the perception of the religious believer. This style of argument shouldn't be applauded. Religious apologists ignore human rights crimes as less important than their theology as a result of this moving the goalposts and they're simply unwilling to listen to any arguments that portray religion as anything else but good in their coherence of the world.[199] Whenever a particular belief in their

---

8. [198] "Moving the Goalposts." *Https://Www.logicallyfallacious.com*, www.logicallyfallacious.com/tools/lp/Bo/LogicalFallacies/129/Moving-the-Goalposts.

9. [199] Kahneman, Daniel. Chapter 6:"Norms, Surprises, and Causes" (71-78). *Thinking, fast and slow*. Farrar, Straus and Giroux, 2015.

religion is rendered untenable in modernity then the reasons for the belief are substituted for different reasons to defend the belief; once the belief is successfully removed then religious apologists argue that such a belief had nothing to do with religion.[200] Homosexual rights is an example of moving the goalposts; some people against homosexuality attempted to substitute their religious reasons with their own ignorant understanding of animals in the wildlife by asserting that homosexuality didn't exist in the animal kingdom. Yet, they were wrong because their understanding of the world and animal biology was uninformed; they substituted their religious reasons for cultural and pseudo-scientific reasons because they wanted to be consistent with their beliefs.[201] The psychological desire for consistency is what led them to substitute their religious reasons for what they ignorantly believed to be credible facts about life.[202] There

---

10. [200] Kahneman, Daniel. Chapter 9: Answering an Easier Question (97-104). *Thinking, fast and slow*. Farrar, Straus and Giroux, 2015.

11. [201] Kahneman, Daniel. Chapter 9: Answering an Easier Question (97-104). *Thinking, fast and slow*. Farrar, Straus and Giroux, 2015.

12. [202] Cialdini, Robert B. Chapter 3: Commitment and Consistency (52-95) *Influence: Science and practice*. 4th ed., 21st Century Bks, 2002.

were always homosexual animals in the animal kingdom but those animals were never mentioned in schools so that parents wouldn't become offended by their children learning about homosexual animals. Once homosexuality is generally accepted, then society shifts its tune to argue that anti-homosexuality is not a true interpretation of the faith.[203]

A third logical fallacy is the "Catch-22 fallacy" of open interpretation and religion itself. Catch-22 refers to a paradoxical situation in which people cannot escape because of contradictory rules.[204] In regards to the Ten Commandments of the Abrahamic faiths, the Commandments are either the inerrant words of God or they are utterly meaningless. Open interpretation creates a theological paradox in which following the rules means you're a religious believer but contradicting the rules still allows you to be a religious

13. [203] "Moving the Goalposts." *Https://Www.logicallyfallacious.com*, www.logicallyfallacious.com/tools/lp/Bo/LogicalFallacies/129/Moving-the-Goalposts.

14. [204] "Circular Reasoning." *Https://Www.logicallyfallacious.com*, www.logicallyfallacious.com/tools/lp/Bo/LogicalFallacies/66/Circular-Reasoning.

believer too.[205] Therefore, following the tenants of a faith or any of the other parables that have moral teachings has no value unless we decide to give them value. It could be argued that the believer who follows a greater degree of the rules is more true to the religious faith but open interpretation is an acceptance of personal preference. Thus, following a greater amount of rules or spending more time on religious activities wouldn't mean a greater or more truthful position of the religious faith. People would be allowed to contradict whatever rules they disliked at any given moment. Religion functions within this framework and people consistently change the contexts of moral teachings to suit themselves. Given this, what value can religion provide in terms of moral teachings? If you're allowed to make any contradictions to moral teachings to suit yourselves then what value is there in believing in your specific God or Gods? What stops people from arguing that not lying or not killing aren't true interpretations of their faith within the societies that they live in? What stops people

---

15. [205] "Circular Reasoning." *Https://Www.logicallyfallacious.com*, www.logicallyfallacious.com/tools/lp/Bo/LogicalFallacies/66/Circular-Reasoning.

from ignoring those precepts if religious beliefs are openly interpretative?

It seems evident that religious teachings don't prevent these consequences. In fact, the silence of religious institutions whenever their nation-state goes to war is a powerful example of 'Thou Shalt Not Kill' having no moral value in the Abrahamic faiths of the predominately Abrahamic countries. If we make distinctions of whom lives and dies based upon national identity and ignore casualties of war as an afterthought, then what does that mean for the so-called immutable laws of God? Whether they are followed or not, people still profess faith and believe themselves to be part of the faith. How can these teachings then be morally good when they ultimately don't matter? Utilizing open interpretation, people are simply moving the goalposts because they change what the meaning behind religious morals is to suit themselves – even to the point of ignoring human rights crimes conducted by their own country. The supposed significance of religious morality changes for the convenience of the religious believer to justify any action or inaction. Bombings, village massacres, and other crimes are conducted upon out-groups of people that are perceived to be of less value in terms of human life than the in-group; this isn't simply combatants but innocent children mercilessly killed in bombings and other atrocities at taxpayer expense.[206] They become an afterthought thanks to the belief in open interpretation and the afterlife; people can conveniently ignore "Thou Shalt Not Kill" in these instances and make themselves feel better by imagining the dead children in the afterlife. Thus, open interpretation helps create self-exalted impotence and apathy towards such crimes against humanity. Within the framework of open interpretation, killing in the name of the religious faith has equal value to not killing in the name of the faith. In practical terms, this is how religious faith is utilized in all nation-states. On what grounds can such a self-contradiction have value?

Implicit Exclusivity

---

16. [206] Hedges, Chris. *War Is a Force That Gives Us Meaning*. PublicAffairs, 2002.

A principal reason why open interpretation has been so successful, despite its glaring flaws, is the implicit belief that only objections within the in-group of a religious faith have value. Out-groups are presumed to be facetious, lacking good morals, lacking depth in analysis, and potentially harboring an insidious intent to besmirch the religious faith.[207] For all intents and purposes, this is a form of tribalism; no matter what the out-group does, they will be regarded with suspicion and derision. Only when a person becomes similar to the in-group will they be welcomed as "open-minded" and thoughtful.[208] That is why it would be more accurate to say narcissistic impulse as opposed to "relatedness" in terms of psychological discourse when discussing how commonality makes people more interested in others.

The extent of the implicit exclusivity can vary from denomination to denomination and person to person but there are

---

17. [207] Ispas, Alexa. *Psychology and politics: a social identity perspective.* Psychology Press, 2014.

18. [208] Cialdini, Robert B. *Influence: Science and practice.* 4th ed., 21st Century Bks, 2002.

certain predisposed beliefs that show strong elements of tribalism. In the context of the Abrahamic faiths, believers often argue and seem to internally feel that their readings of the Abrahamic texts are more accurate than an atheist reading them. To the perception of the religious believer, a belief in God confers a greater amount of understanding of Biblical passages. Yet, research by Pew Research has indicated that most atheists have a greater understanding of the contents of the holy books of their prior religion and they have a greater knowledge of religion in general than theists.[209] To an outside observer, the claim of religious books having more accurate or special qualities is simply an indication that the believers find the passages to be more meaningful without critical analysis.[210] An ex-Christian penpal from Australia once informed me, when I asked him about his prior beliefs, that his fellow Christians simply believed that the Bible

---

19. [209] "U.S. Religious Knowledge Survey." *Pew Research Center's Religion & Public Life Project*, Pew Research Center's Religion & Public Life Project, 19 Dec. 2017, www.pewforum.org/2010/09/28/u-s-religious-knowledge-survey/.

20. [210] Kahneman, Daniel. Chapter 4: The Associative Machine (50-58) and Chapter 5: Cognitive Ease (59-70). *Thinking, fast and slow*. Farrar, Straus and Giroux, 2015.

had magic words that only fellow Christians could understand and that the special magical qualities of the Bible disappeared when non-believers tried to read them.[211] According to him, they believed in some holy qualities that only they could understand. The exclusivity is further solidified through regarding other faiths as fooled into believing in falsehoods or practicing some form of "evil" worship. Other faiths would argue the same of them; especially in the context of Abrahamic religions and thus permanent in-group and out-group implications would exist to divide people.[212][213]

Moral Neutrality

Theistic arguments in favor of being morally neutral to killings during war reveal a depth of apathy and savagery that disprove the supposed innate goodness of religious morals. In

21. [211] Kahneman, Daniel. *Thinking, fast and slow*. Farrar, Straus and Giroux, 2015.

22. [212] Ispas, Alexa. *Psychology and politics: a social identity perspective*. Psychology Press, 2014.

23. [213] Cialdini, Robert B. *Influence: Science and practice*. 4th ed., 21st Century Bks, 2002.

practical effect, the immutable laws of God stop outside of national

borders and the people within those borders ignore the war crimes of

their nation-state. The attempts to argue that such topics are "too

complex" shows both the weakness of religious morality when

applied to reality and the true level of apathy that people have for

other human beings perceived as out-groups.[214] A desire to remain

innocent of wrongdoing seems to become a desire to be innocent from

any responsibility. The real life apathy seems to be instilled from

cultural depictions of heroes and protagonists being innocent of moral

wrongdoing to convey the desire to live in an unrealistic world with

no responsibility – children's TV shows that teach such lessons infer

the desire to live in a patently unrealistic lifestyle and worsen the

ability of adapting complex thoughts when children become adults.

The notion of soldiers from their nation-state committing war

atrocities, such as war rapes and the mass murders of civilians, can't

be handled well in a religious believer's coherence of the world. As a

result, through a combination of moral neutrality and good versus

---

24. [214] McDermott, Rose. *Political Psychology in International Relations*. Ann Arbor: U of Michigan, 2004. Print

evil, some adults perceive all things outside of their oversimplifications of the world as evil and begin to suppress a nihilistic viewpoint. The oversimplified perspective helps apologists defend war atrocities that were committed via the inculcation of revering religious systems that promote warfare; religious passages become tools of manipulation to comfort people who learn of human rights crimes by insisting that an intrinsic failure in human nature is to blame. The dead victims become an afterthought that is ignored for the comfort of the religious believer.

Moral neutrality is an attempt to absolve all forms of violence and actions commonly asserted as "evil" by Abrahamic morality itself. Moral neutrality ignores the effects and focuses strictly on the personal ego of the one committing human rights crimes. When religious morality is needed the most, its interpretation is changed and violence is permitted. Instead of focusing upon the lives of innocents being mercilessly slaughtered, non-sequitur analogies about surgeons cutting into a body are utilized to manipulate people into killing other human beings to promote a war campaign.[215] Unrealistic belief

systems serve as a comfort for the killers as they slaughter innocent

lives – including children. Minimizing moral question to terms of

"intentions" reveals a total apathy for life itself.[216] Arguing in favor of

a religious cause, like regaining religious lands, as the reason for

brutal acts of cruelty and stupidity shows the innate emptiness in

believing that religion is a force of goodness.[217] All human rights

crimes can be ignored for the sake of a recovering religious lands and

property. The value of human life is less valuable to fellow humans

than religious iconography and religious land; religious believers

profess the truth and peacefulness of their specific religion during

missionary outings after slaughtering people within the region under

25. [215] Abels, Richard. "Crusades and early Christian attitudes toward warfare." *Academia.edu - Share research*, www.academia.edu/22844402/Crusades_and_early_Christian_attitudes_to ward_warfare.

26. [216] Abels, Richard. "Crusades and early Christian attitudes toward warfare." *Academia.edu - Share research*, www.academia.edu/22844402/Crusades_and_early_Christian_attitudes_to ward_warfare.

27. [217] Abels, Richard. "Crusades and early Christian attitudes toward warfare." *Academia.edu - Share research*, www.academia.edu/22844402/Crusades_and_early_Christian_attitudes_to ward_warfare.

the justification of the religion itself.[218] Moreover, the slaughter is usually justified by bringing God to the savages; such are the cases of the Christian Crusades, the genocide of the Native Americans, the genocide of the Philippines, the colonization of India by a Portugal inquisition, and the genocide of the Tasmanian aboriginals. The lives of victims become part of "history" and no longer have any value because it happened years ago but sacrifices in the name of the religion should be celebrated forever. It is a selective system that only seeks narcissistic self-worship of the in-group religious identity and ignores the innocents who were slaughtered because they're an out-group.[219][220][221]

---

28. [218] Abels, Richard. "Crusades and early Christian attitudes toward warfare." *Academia.edu - Share research*, www.academia.edu/22844402/Crusades_and_early_Christian_attitudes_toward_warfare.

29. [219] Ispas, Alexa. *Psychology and politics: a social identity perspective*. Psychology Press, 2014.

30. [220] Kahneman, Daniel. Chapter 4: The Associative Machine (50-58) and Chapter 5: Cognitive Ease (59-70). *Thinking, fast and slow*. Farrar, Straus and Giroux, 2015.

31. [221] Hedges, Chris. *War Is a Force That Gives Us Meaning*. PublicAffairs, 2002.

Just War Theory and Moral Relativism

All attempts at defining "Just War Theory" – an argument that historically originated from theological arguments to defend wars[222] – has been a mere obfuscation to defend the political and economic objectives of a nation-state that goes to warfare with others. It reduces sensory warfare; bombing campaigns, killings of entire villages, war rapes, child soldiers, child killings, and ethnic cleansing into sophistry about fictitious intentions that had no bearing on going to warfare.[223] It reduces human rights as less valuable than sovereign objectives and it is mostly untrue of war operations conducted in foreign countries because war operations usually require long-term planning for success. Prolonged war is likely because the foreign government and civilians feel their sovereign territory is in danger; thus they will always argue self-defense against foreign incursion. Obtaining

32. [222] Abels, Richard. "Crusades and early Christian attitudes toward warfare." *Academia.edu - Share research*, www.academia.edu/22844402/Crusades_and_early_Christian_attitudes_toward_warfare.

33. [223] Hedges, Chris. *War Is a Force That Gives Us Meaning*. PublicAffairs, 2002.

military objectives effectively requires bombing campaigns and mass raids that endanger civilians. For all the lauded goodness of religion, it unalterably fails to stop any wars and has deep theological pretexts to justify them. Religion will never be the end of war because it creates fictional notions about God, Gods, a flimsy morality, and the afterlife to justify war's barbaric nature.

Religious teachings within national borders practice a more absolute form of moral teachings about not killing but outside of national borders it ubiquitously concedes to moral relativism. In all practical sense, what can the notion of "moral neutrality" under religion be called besides moral relativism itself? Most apologists make arguments from semantics or use religious teachings and metaphysical beliefs to ignore mass killings conducted by their nation-state upon civilians in other nation-states. Anchoring our view to the intent of the national leader, of which we couldn't possibly know and historically has used deceit to bring forth horrific consequences, depicts the utter failings of religious morality and the willful ignorance of scholars who defend it. If we reduce mass violence into terms of intentions; we reduce massive death tolls to the personal preference of our leader's ego. Moreover, what prevents a foreign nation-state from justifying bombings, killings, war rapes, and other forms of human cruelty upon us under the Just War Theory's terms of intentions? The foreign people could easily defend the death and destruction that they've inflicted our people under the justification of their leader's intentions being genuinely good. Or they could argue that minimizing casualties inflicted upon us was for the sake of their objective. Why couldn't they also argue that our dead are in some form of afterlife and thus we should feel less despondent about our losses? I'd rather not get into arguments for reprisal against wrongdoings because that is how Osama bin Laden justified 9/11; he argued US bombings in different locations upon Muslim civilians, the aid in funding Israel's wars on Palestine, the collusion with Islamic dictators who sell oil on the US dollar, and the sanctions on Iraq that killed approximately 500,000 innocent children justified his terrorism in his letter to the US.[224][225]

---

34. [224] "Full text: bin Laden's 'letter to America'." *The Guardian*, Guardian

Psychological studies have found that people behave reciprocally with other people; meaning if you do a kind gesture then they are likely to return a gesture of kindness and if you commit an egregious act then they're likely to do the same.[226] Religious lessons of being peaceful have never held-up to real life standards because of the constant reinterpretations of religion throughout human history. That isn't an indictment against human nature; it's a total moral failing of religion's claim of being the ultimate truth and teaching good morals. The divine moral codes always need to be changed so the nation-state can meet its objectives.[227] Killing people – including innocent children – becomes ignored through religious teachings. Religious teachings help to comfort the killers with the idea of human

News and Media, 24 Nov. 2002, www.theguardian.com/world/2002/nov/24/theobserver.

35. [225] Gause, F. Gregory . "Getting It Backward on Iraq." *Foreign Affairs*, Foreign Affairs, 28 Jan. 2009, www.foreignaffairs.com/articles/iraq/1999-05-01/getting-it-backward-iraq.

36. [226] Cialdini, Robert B. Chapter 2: Reciprocation (19-50). *Influence: Science and practice*. 4th ed., 21st Century Bks, 2002.

37. [227] Kahneman, Daniel. *Thinking, fast and slow*. Farrar, Straus and Giroux, 2015.

nature being synonymous with failure and evil.[228] Civilians who feel empathetic for the human rights atrocities use religion as a scapegoat by telling themselves that any dead civilians, such as murdered children, are in the afterlife and that the politicians who promoted the war will be in a negative version of the afterlife; these beliefs are to make themselves feel better and to more effectively ignore the atrocities. Therefore, religion does more to excuse egregious acts of violence and doesn't instill good life lessons.

Control

A significant factor in the historic reinterpretation of religious teachings, particularly after political changes, is the need for control over their own lives. People have biological need for control in order to feel that their actions matter and to keep a coherent worldview that makes sense to them. Psychological research has shown the belief that our actions have an impact significantly reduces anxiety, laziness,

---

38. [228] Kahneman, Daniel. *Thinking, fast and slow*. Farrar, Straus and Giroux, 2015.

167

pessimism, and fear of the world.[229] That is why we create our own "causes" for events and why the fallacy of "causation doesn't equal correlation" run rampant in many arguments regarding political topics.[230] This need for control can become dangerous because it leads to using a scapegoat to explain disasters; an example would be how the war reparations upon Germany after the end of World War 1 combined with the economic depression resulted in Christian extremism that led to the genocide of six million people comprised of the minority groups of Germany. A modern example would be the fear and hatred of Muslim Americans within the US after the attack on the Twin Towers on September 11th, 2001. (Note: I would also like to mention that I am not arguing moral equivalence between the Holocaust and 9/11 or the genocide of the Jews to the discrimination of a subset of Americans.) The belief in removing the "undesirables" from society occurs because people make rash judgments on how to

---

39. [229] Kahneman, Daniel. *Thinking, fast and slow*. Farrar, Straus and Giroux, 2015.

40. [230] Kahneman, Daniel. Chapter 6:"Norms, Surprises, and Causes" (71-78) and Chapter 7: A Machine for Jumping to Conclusions (79-88). *Thinking, fast and slow*. Farrar, Straus and Giroux, 2015.

remove the violence from being inflicted upon their in-group.[231][232]

They begin to perceive minority groups similar to the attackers as intrinsically associated with them and create caricatures that fuel the coherence of the out-group being pure evil. There is usually a rash overestimation of how many of the minority groups harbor extremist ideologies to justify discrimination and stricter policies. These policies are implemented because people believe it will contain or control the threat without any clear analysis on the real causes of violence through statistical research or proper studies of the views that terrorists actually hold.

Argument of First Cause

The first cause argument is the most notorious use of the God of the gaps argument; that is, the fallacy in which the unknown parts of a subject matter has God substituted as the explanation when science has yet to discover the answer to an issue. This is primarily

41. [231] Cialdini, Robert B. Chapter 1: Weapons of Influence (1-16). *Influence: Science and practice*. 4th ed., 21st Century Bks, 2002.

42. [232] McDermott, Rose. *Political Psychology in International Relations*. Ann Arbor: U of Michigan, 2004. Print.

used by theists to try to find a coherent balance between religion and science to satisfy their own doubts about faith. In the case of First Cause, the argument is that there must be a Creator deity because something cannot come from nothing and that the life wouldn't be able to exist without a Creator deity with a divine intent and purpose. Within the context of this belief is the argument that randomness or spontaneity cannot form the basis for a cause and that human life is largely following the trajectory of a Creator deity's guiding hand because of how the world is organized. Since all of life and the universe has a beginning, then the beginning must be a Creator deity and this view has been adapted into modern forms such as Fine-Tuning.

As a side note, I profusely apologize to any Biologist, Cosmologist, astrophysicist, theoretical physicist, or any other scientist in the various Natural Sciences for misattributing or misapplying the science, if I have done so. For the purposes of addressing the First Cause argument, I think some oversimplification is needed since science is a multifarious and complex subject.

For this section, I'll largely be referencing John Stuart Mill's profound argument against First Cause in conjunction with my limited knowledge of the latest scientific insights into the origins of the universe found by modern scientific research. I've broken it down to four numerical propositions to get the root of the issue. I feel that attacking the central assumptions on this matter is key.

1. The belief in God presupposes knowledge that people simply do not have of the observable and natural world.[233] Arguments from faith are matters of intuition and anecdotal inference that lack empirical evidence on the basis of an origin. The closest understanding to the origin would be the mathematical calculations provided by astrophysicists, which have recently developed a mathematical proof that the universe could have come from nothing.[234]

---

43. [233] Mill, John Stuart. *Three essays on religion*. Timeless Wisdom Collection, 2016.

44. [234] "A Mathematical Proof That The Universe Could Have Formed Spontaneously From Nothing." *Medium*, The Physics ArXiv Blog, 11 Apr. 2014, medium.com/the-physics-arxiv-blog/a-mathematical-proof-that-the-universe-could-have-formed-spontaneously-from-nothing-ed7ed0f304a3.

2. The reasoning of *a priori* doesn't prove a God's existence. What people assume to follow as a logical transition is looking back at the past through a succession of changes from the standpoint of the present civilization that they inhabit.[235] However, what they're actually doing is looking at the origin of composition that our species utilized to invent more complex devices.[236] Inferring a Creator on the basis of the original composition doesn't have a logical transition behind it because it is just human creativity to form complex systems specifically to serve a purpose for the betterment of human civilizations. Proponents for First Cause take the transition as a given, such as the circular reasoning that it cannot conceivably be any other way, when it's not. It's never been an organized transition toward the fateful present; it's only been changes as a result of human agency working to alter and modify their systems of organization through inventions or new government systems. It doesn't acknowledge regress as a result of humans stubbornly holding to

45. [235] Mill, John Stuart. *Three essays on religion.* Timeless Wisdom Collection, 2016.

46. [236] Mill, John Stuart. *Three essays on religion.* Timeless Wisdom Collection, 2016.

traditions or abandoning attempts at positive change in favor of ignorance or apathy towards potent social issues, which largely come from religion itself. In fact, the general idea doesn't factor failed civilizations, fallen empires, or abusive practices like the eugenics movement that harm people and are then ignored when teaching history.

3. While human civilizations exist due to a lengthy period of changes as a result of human agency, human biology and the biology of other animals largely follows from a progression that is contradictory to the existence of a Creator deity. The belief that a being of high intellect and power preceded us doesn't follow the logical order of the world through natural selection of biology because the assumptions misunderstand what natural selection is. There is no reason to assume a higher being made anything. The logical consequence of our observations of the natural world form a general theory that more basic compositions created an organized composition greater than itself into a higher composition from mutations in order to increase its survivability[237]; we logically are the product of such a long period of composition growing into higher composition through natural selection from gene mutations increasing our survivability over long periods of time. The human body is a complex organism, it's very organs harboring complex systems that exist in service of keeping a human body alive and functioning. Our genetic ancestors seem ridiculous to us because our evolution allowed for us to improve from our origins. From microbes to higher forms of life like birds, apes, and us. Therefore, from the standpoint of both *a priori* and empiricism, we came from lesser parts to make a greater whole through the long history of evolution.[238] But what about animals who became lower in form due to genetic mutations, such as some dinosaurs? As mentioned, the gene mutations inherited by offspring help increase their survivability over time; the pertinent concept to understand is which genetic mutations help increase the species

---

47. [237] Mill, John Stuart. *Three essays on religion*. Timeless Wisdom Collection, 2016.

48. [238] Mill, John Stuart. *Three essays on religion*. Timeless Wisdom Collection, 2016.

survival. Therefore, genetic mutations slowly change the species by allowing those who can adapt to new conditions to propagate more offspring.

4. Following from three in understanding changing composition, the only permanent, simplistic answer and origin of composition is the *Law of Conservation of Mass-Energy Equivalence* and this doesn't need a higher power. We're simply thinking of *a priori* wrong when advocating for a divine being as our origin when we base our assessment on anecdotal inference to the world around us. The most simplistic answer is the *Law of Conservation of Mass-Energy Equivalence*. Mass-energy is the same. It goes through changes in their elementary properties into higher organizational forms through eons of transition.[239] There's no need for a Creator or First Cause in that process at all, because its misunderstanding cosmology. Judging from the evidence, the universe may have always existed and the "start" of the universe that theoretical models detail may just be a change in composition as per the *Law of Conservation of Mass-*

49. [239] Mill, John Stuart. *Three essays on religion*. Timeless Wisdom Collection, 2016.

Energy. Therefore, there is no need for the existence of a Creator deity.

Control, Communalism, and Fine Tuning

Before the rise of science, religion was used to interpret phenomena under forms of communalism. Under ancient Abrahamic tribes: mental illness was seen as witchcraft or devilry, disease was seen as the wrath of God, failed crops or dangerous weather was seen as the wrath of God, luck was seen as a blessing, victory of one barbaric tribe over other barbaric tribes was seen as God having chosen the people to succeed, failure against another tribe was seen as God's punishment upon them for some miscellaneous violation of ancient religious ethics, and concepts such as sinfulness in human nature and blasphemy were attempts at creating a convincing worldview.[240][241] It was a worldview that explained weather patterns,

---

50. [240] Kahneman, Daniel. *Thinking, fast and slow*. Farrar, Straus and Giroux, 2015.

disease, success, failure, and luck as part of the ancient community's actions so that they felt a sense of control over their situation.[242][243] Incidentally, desperation is known to increase less cognizant and fanciful worldviews in order to find an escape from suffering or to blame it upon another group of peoples – such as the history of anti-Semitism throughout Christianity and Islam or the destruction of other tribes throughout the Old Testament.

Modern religion still has instances of interpreting lucky events as religious phenomena but it has mostly been used to selectively pick and choose events for a worldview that fits the idea of a specific creator deity. The argument of "fine tuning", that is the idea of the universe being guided by a divine hand because of the uniqueness of the earth and the human race, and the antipathy toward the idea that

51. [241] Cialdini, Robert B. Chapter 4: Social Proof (98-140). *Influence: Science and practice.* 4th ed., 21st Century Bks, 2002.

52. [242] Cialdini, Robert B. Chapter 4: Social Proof (98-140). *Influence: Science and practice.* 4th ed., 21st Century Bks, 2002.

53. [243] Kahneman, Daniel. *Thinking, fast and slow.* Farrar, Straus and Giroux, 2015.

the universe could come from nothing have been soundly rejected because of recent scientific discoveries and mathematical probabilities; the universe doesn't need a self-caused or eternal deity and it is mathematically probable that the universe could have come from nothing.[244] Moreover, there are earth-like planets in the habitable zones of the universe, of which the earth is one planet of many, so the earth isn't unique as religious believers tend to argue. Many reject string theory and the concept of a universe coming from nothing, despite the mathematical feasibility of the universe coming from nothing, on the basis of its cold indifference to the existence of the human race. Their personal incredulity is a fallacy and isn't a positive argument in favor of a higher power. Furthermore, it would be entirely fallacious to argue that mathematics doesn't have a basis in our personal lives. Math is not some cold and invisible part of our lives; it is something we constantly take for granted. Subject matters such as population size, the speed of an internet connection, the

54. [244] "A Mathematical Proof That The Universe Could Have Formed Spontaneously From Nothing." *Medium*, The Physics ArXiv Blog, 11 Apr. 2014, medium.com/the-physics-arxiv-blog/a-mathematical-proof-that-the-universe-could-have-formed-spontaneously-from-nothing-ed7ed0f304a3.

amount of laps or repetitions for quality exercise, dieting, surgeries to save our lives, and the correct dosage for ingestion of quality medicine are all daily and complex forms of mathematics in our personal lives. It is not miracles, but human ingenuity in progressing mathematics in conjunction with biology, computer science, computer engineering, physics, modernized medical practices, and other scientific-mathematical subjects that has allowed us to live quality lifestyles and increase our life expectancy.

It has been religion that has had to concede to modernity by using the "God of the gaps" as the basis for arguments such as fine tuning and for there being a "cause" for the creation of the universe; the use of God where science still hasn't determined factors of how the universe works is not just an argument from ignorance but theological-induced blindness from the axioms of religious faith. Theological-induced blindness is similar to theory-induced blindness; people anchor their worldview upon a specific theory from a specific set of beliefs and ignore the exceptions as strange occurrences instead of accepting the weaknesses of the theory; thereby ignoring the factors and factual information where the theory cannot be applied.[245] The God of the gaps is a modern attempt at understanding the rest of the world through human iconography, by trying to relate the facts of the universe to our existence as humans.[246] Concepts such as the God of the gaps are a narcissistic desire by humanity to be the most important aspect of the universe. Untenable aspects of holy texts like Adam and Eve, Manu, The Abrahamic God creating the world in seven days, Noah's Ark, and similar fanciful ideas have been rendered unable to be interpreted as truthful; leaving vast swathes of these texts as symbolic or metaphorical instead of being interpreted literally as people in ancient societies understood them to be. Ergo, they no longer give humanity any objective value and don't have any truths beyond what we want them to be.

The argument for fine tuning, the use of the God of the gaps, has been thoroughly discredited for many years. A mathematical

---

55. [245] Kahneman, Daniel. Chapter 27: The Prospect Theory (278-288). *Thinking, fast and slow*. Farrar, Straus and Giroux, 2015.

56. [246] Kahneman, Daniel. *Thinking, fast and slow*. Farrar, Straus and Giroux, 2015.

proof has found that it is realistically possible that the universe came from nothingness and the earth is among many earth-like planets to exist in a habitable zone of the universe. Even before these discoveries, the argument from fine tuning was absurd. It posited that the universe needed a cause and that the cause had to be "willing", yet that is a total non-sequitur. A cause does not have to be willing to do anything; furthermore the fine tuning argument used the natural laws of the universe as an attempt to validate itself. This was under the belief that the natural laws couldn't be random otherwise nothing could be consistent or exist on any consistent basis. If they already concede that the natural laws of the universe are true, then why believe that the natural laws of the universe were suspended twice for the sake of Jesus? Even if there was a creator deity, that wouldn't have proven that Jesus Christ was who he claimed to be or that he harbored the ability to suspend the natural laws of the universe. The same applies to other religious beliefs.

From an outside view, it is easy to see what the pious are desperately attempting to do. They have attempted to reorganize and reframe the scientific studies of the big bang, the expanding universe, and the events before the big bang with their preconceived biases through their misrepresentation of the facts. We humans seek meaning in our lives and we're biased to look for "causes" to create a coherent worldview about ourselves.[247] Due to the human bias of looking for causes as an explanation, the pious have sought to find a "cause" for the big bang that they have construed to be similar to their biblical deity. Yet, just because people desire to find a cause doesn't mean that one actually exists and people are predisposed to finding false causes for events that create stories in their minds that make them feel good instead of assessing evidence for their beliefs.[248] The pious that use the fine tuning argument wish to be consistent with their prior beliefs and try to create a coherent view that they're more

57. [247] Kahneman, Daniel. Chapter 6:"Norms, Surprises, and Causes" (71-78) and Chapter 7: A Machine for Jumping to Conclusions (79-88). *Thinking, fast and slow*. Farrar, Straus and Giroux, 2015.

58. [248] Kahneman, Daniel. *Thinking, fast and slow*. Farrar, Straus and Giroux, 2015.

familiar with.[249] The gaps in the fine tuning argument are numerous: why did a creator deity not make the universe more habitable for human life beyond the miniscule habitable zone? If the heat death of the universe due to rapid expansion is going to happen, and the current scientific data suggests that it will, then why did a creator deity make the universe only for our species to eventually die once the heat dissipates from the universe? If the universe was made with humanity in mind, then why make it so difficult for us to live outside of the earth?

Incidentally, much of the higher forms of life before us have also fallen into extinction and thus contradict the notion of a divine plan. If the purpose of a divine plan is narrowly focused intentions upon humans, then why bother bringing into existence and then exterminating entire species of animals that existed before we humans did? Why even create the dinosaurs, or any other animal species, that isn't governed by theistic laws and have no effect upon them? What

59. [249] Cialdini, Robert B. Chapter 3: Commitment and Consistency (52-95) *Influence: Science and practice*. 4th ed., 21st Century Bks, 2002.

purpose does it serve humans for a God to give life to and then exterminate entire species of animals that have no tangible connection to us? Did the entirety of their species simply exist to be harvested as sacrifices to pose as a warning for human arrogance? For instance, assuming the Abrahamic religions are true, and the Abrahamic God exists and acknowledging the fact that animals cannot commit sins because they hold no capacity to understand human morals; then the Abrahamic God wiped out a large and diverse set of species, the dinosaurs, without sinfulness playing a factor in their annihilation. There was no judgment of good or evil, the Abrahamic God simply wiped out a species with no moral judgments intended, there was no greater divine purpose for their existence, and sinful conduct was a total non-factor. What was the point? What purpose did it serve humans to have done this? If the Abrahamic God did it to bring fear for human arrogance or for no reason at all, then how can the Abrahamic God not be recognized as cruel and using life itself as merely a plaything? If the Abrahamic God is innately good, then what purpose could bringing to life and wiping out a species with no relation to original sin serve?

Even disregarding these arguments as part of God's mysterious plan, and even disregarding the genuine likelihood that the universe can come from nothingness, the supposition of a creator deity is an unsubstantiated assumption and its existence would need to be substantiated to show that it was more likely than any other baseless assumption about what came before the big bang. For example, I could postulate the assumption of Friedrich Nietzsche's thought experiment of eternal recurrence as the event before the big bang.

For those unfamiliar with the eternal occurrence thought experiment of Friedrich Nietzsche's from his book, *The Gay Science*:

"The Heaviest Burden. What if a demon crept after you into your loneliest loneliness some day or night, and said to you: "This life, as you live it at present, and have lived it, you must live it once more, and also innumerable times; and there will be nothing new in it, but every pain and every joy and every thought and every sigh, and all the unspeakably small and great in thy life must come to you again, and all in the same series and sequence - and similarly this spider and this moonlight among the trees, and similarly this moment, and I myself. The eternal sand-glass of existence will

ever be turned once more, and you with it, you speck of dust!" - Would you not throw yourself down and gnash your teeth, and curse the demon that so spoke? Or have you once experienced a tremendous moment in which you would answer him: "You are a God, and never did I hear anything so divine!" If that thought acquired power over you as you are, it would transform you, and perhaps crush you; the question with regard to all and everything: "Do you want this once more, and also for innumerable times?" would lie as the heaviest burden upon your activity! Or, how would you have to become favourably inclined to yourself and to life, so as to long for nothing more ardently than for this last eternal sanctioning and sealing?"[250]

Can you prove my assumption that eternal recurrence occurred before the big bang is wrong? No, and you wouldn't need to because I haven't provided any evidence that eternal recurrence is possible. The unlikelihood of life coming into existence doesn't prove eternal recurrence just as the unlikelihood doesn't prove the fine tuning argument. Eternal recurrence is equally as valid as a creator deity being a cause for the universe; in other words, highly improbable and based more on fanciful belief than empirical evidence.

If you believe in the fine tuning argument then consider what it would mean if eternal recurrence was real; what if, upon the death of the universe, the universe brought itself back from nothingness and

---

60. [250] Nietzsche, Friedrich Wilhelm. *The gay science (the joyful wisdom)*. Edited by Oscar Levy. Translated by Thomas Common, #52881, Gutenberg, 2016, www.gutenberg.org/files/52881/52881-h/52881-h.htm.

goes through the same cycle eternally like a clock. What if after your death, you eventually go through the same life experiences with no changes. You are born the same as you were, you go through the exact same experiences in your life. Everything that you did and will do will be repeated forever with no changes. Every mistake, every regret, every tragedy, every joy, every triumph, every loving moment, and so forth will be constantly repeated and you will have to relive all of your experiences with no changes for all of eternity. You will have no memory of repeating your life and you will exist like this for all eternity. What if that is the reality of the universe? What if you will endure all of your life's choices for eternity? How do you feel about it and does it change what you want to do at the present moment of your life? What can you do in this moment to make yourself satisfied with the prospect of living your life eternally? And, if this assumption were the reality of the universe and your life, would God be worth anything to you anymore?

Doubt

Historically, doubt was regarded as sinful and punishable within the Abrahamic faiths. Modernity has rendered blasphemy laws obsolete; religion has fractured into several religious denominations in a large part due to valuing freedom of speech and the consequences of having different interpretations on supernatural phenomena. Thus, doubt itself is no longer seen as an act synonymous with so-called evil intentions or evil thoughts. Modernity rendered such a belief untenable in first world countries. Religious believers, in an attempt to reconcile the spread of doubt, have reinterpreted doubt to mean the proof of imperfections and arrogance of humans in trying to understand what is beyond human comprehension.[251] It is argued the intrinsic imperfection of humanity causes doubt and that reaffirming one's faith despite doubt shows a true conviction for faith and for love

---

61. [251] Baird, Julia. "Doubt as a Sign of Faith." *The New York Times*, The New York Times, 25 Sept. 2014, www.nytimes.com/2014/09/26/opinion/julia-baird-doubt-as-a-sign-of-faith.html.

of God.[252] It is perceived to be a commitment and relationship with God in spite of the shortcomings of humanity.[253]

While it seems to express a degree of humility and innocence on the part of religious believers, all it truly does is create a win-win situation for the convenience of the religious believer. Construing doubt as a form of faith is a logical fallacy called circular reasoning because faith in God no longer matters under the "humility of doubt" argument.[254] Essentially, doubting God's existence is reinterpreted as being genuine in your faith in God because of your human weakness.[255] It is a paradoxical belief, if you have faith then you are a

62. [252] Baird, Julia. "Doubt as a Sign of Faith." *The New York Times*, The New York Times, 25 Sept. 2014, www.nytimes.com/2014/09/26/opinion/julia-baird-doubt-as-a-sign-of-faith.html.

63. [253] Baird, Julia. "Doubt as a Sign of Faith." *The New York Times*, The New York Times, 25 Sept. 2014, www.nytimes.com/2014/09/26/opinion/julia-baird-doubt-as-a-sign-of-faith.html.

64. [254] Lane, Christopher. "Losing Our Religion: Why Doubt Is a Passionate Exercise." *Psychology Today*, Sussex Publishers, 20 May 2011, www.psychologytoday.com/blog/side-effects/201105/losing-our-religion-why-doubt-is-passionate-exercise.

65. [255] Lane, Christopher. "Losing Our Religion: Why Doubt Is a Passionate Exercise." *Psychology Today*, Sussex Publishers, 20 May 2011, www.psychologytoday.com/blog/side-effects/201105/losing-our-religion-why-doubt-is-passionate-exercise.

true believer and if you don't have faith then you are a true believer under this theological reasoning.[256] It is a self-celebrating logical fallacy; you are a hero no matter what you do or how you actually feel. Thus, having faith in God is irrelevant to the religious believer despite the clear contradiction.

This sort of reasoning ultimately inflicts self-deprecation and celebrates self-contempt as morally good. Your doubts may make you despise your lack of faith; you may view your shortcoming as a personal failure and view yourself negatively because you aren't "perfect" enough to worship your God fully. The defense that people are "only human" when exhibiting or internally admitting doubts is a tacit admittance to misanthropy. To defend the lack of faith, people despise their so-called limitations of being human.[257] People must reaffirm their faith by apologizing to God for being a human being

---

66. [256] "Circular Reasoning." *Https://Www.logicallyfallacious.com*, www.logicallyfallacious.com/tools/lp/Bo/LogicalFallacies/66/Circular-Reasoning.

67. [257] Baird, Julia. "Doubt as a Sign of Faith." *The New York Times*, The New York Times, 25 Sept. 2014, www.nytimes.com/2014/09/26/opinion/julia-baird-doubt-as-a-sign-of-faith.html.

who has intrusive thoughts and opinions outside of a prescribed holy book of morals. While it may seem like humility, it is ultimately a defeatist notion that condemns our humanity as a constant failure compared to the so-called perfection of a God. We must continue, as human beings, to prostrate ourselves and condemn ourselves so that God forgives us for being a human being. Admitting how weak and pitiful we are, mental self-lacerations imposed upon ourselves, is thus a "freedom" of accepting God's will.[258] The statement of "being human" reduces humanity to a state of failure and grief. It is a self-deluded misanthropy because of its inability to attain an unrealistic concept of perfection – a "commitment" to ignoring how theology doesn't fit with reality.[259] Thus, it is intrinsically unhealthy for our state of mind.

Please consider the following: doubt isn't your personal failings or temptation. Doubt is allowing you to view the world

---

68. [258] Cialdini, Robert B. Chapter 3: Commitment and Consistency (52-95) and Authority (178-200). *Influence: Science and practice.* 4th ed., 21st Century Bks, 2002.

69. [259] Cialdini, Robert B. Chapter 3: Commitment and Consistency (52-95). *Influence: Science and practice.* 4th ed., 21st Century Bks, 2002.

outside of theological-induced blindness and unknowingly fighting against the self-hate imposed by religious teachings and practices. *If you have doubt, then you're only sometimes a religious believer and sometimes an atheist.* Doubt is flourishing because people have faith for the sake of their own convenience and modernity is slowly removing the need for religion. Your doubt could also be a desire to observe the world without theological-induced blindness in your personal life because you may no longer want to feel restricted by purportedly cosmic rules. Having uncertainty isn't wrong and it might be a desire for rationality. People can have faith in a multitude of subjects but it is better to have faith in subject matter that is testable and verifiable so as not to deceive ourselves because we don't like the implications of non-belief. Lastly, praising doubt is the faintest of praises because people are essentially admitting that they need to be an atheist at certain times to continue living in modernity and dealing with real world issues.

Chapter 5: Gender Roles

Religion plays an important component in gender roles both historically and within the context of modern society. Throughout human history, feminist campaigns have sought to highlight the struggle of women against religious oppression of their freedom of choice. Basic freedoms such as learning to read and contemporary freedoms such as abortion are the cornerstone of debate throughout the world. However, what are given less focus are the damaging social stigmas upon men. Therefore, this chapter will endeavor to criticize the negatives of both societal gender roles.

Manliness: Psychopathic Self-deprecation

While the idea of masculinity is associated with culture, the axioms of manliness come from religious teachings about the appropriate gender role of men. Men are the "breadwinners" that support the family, discipline the children, and teach respect for authority. Men are taught to be "strong" or "macho" by not showing emotional weakness and the act of crying is perceived to be a total failure of manliness.[260] Anger is perceived as more acceptable for a man compared to the more shameful action of crying under such a belief.[261] Men are taught to act "respectably" by not "giving in" to a notion of promiscuous behavior with women; a woman who is open about sex should be distrusted because she isn't following her gender role of being "loyal" to men. Men are taught that they have intrinsic sexual desire, but the actual desire for sex is something they need to seek forgiveness for because it's synonymous with evil intent. Men must apologize to a higher power for the crime of having biological sexual urges and healthy sexual thoughts. The pursuit of sexual gratification – of self-pleasure and sex with a willing participant – is seen as shameful and men begin to believe that having a cold, indifferent attitude is the sign of being a good man. Their sexual desire, perceived as wicked but intrinsic in their behavior, makes them believe that they have an irresistibly evil component within

1. [260] Green, Laci. "TOXIC MASCULINITY!" *YouTube*, YouTube, 20 Dec. 2017, www.youtube.com/watch?v=i5juyXjDnJ0.

2. [261] Green, Laci. "TOXIC MASCULINITY!" *YouTube*, YouTube, 20 Dec. 2017, www.youtube.com/watch?v=i5juyXjDnJ0.

them that they must act on to be considered manly. Men under this moral belief system are taught to laugh and enjoy photos of nude women online but also feel ashamed with themselves for being so wicked; they try to justify such shame with the idea of male toughness because they're taught that manliness is a form of good moral behavior for men. Interestingly enough, sex psychologists and psychoanalysts have found that men who constantly seek sex from their partner don't do so for just physical reasons; most men who believe in "manliness" think they can only express their tender and emotional side through sex. Otherwise, they must either despise their natural biological processes or be coldly indifferent to what others think of their behavior; they often do both in a strange contradiction by acting tough while condemning their own sexual liberation.

This belief system is mental self-torture and encourages violent suicide. For some men, when they fail at upholding the so-called cornerstone of manliness; of being providers for their family, providing money with a secure job, being "strong" i.e. being emotionless as men, being "tough" about feeling pain, and feeling constant shame for their sexual desires then they seek suicide as a reprieve from the shame of being a failure by not measuring up to those standards.[262] This male stereotype is probably one of the worst developments in all of humankind; not only does it condemn women into feeling ashamed of their bodies by men who then objectify them, but it condemns men into feeling constant regret and shame too. Under the veneer of "good moral teachings" from religion, it creates a systemic culture of self-contempt and self-lassitude by demanding men conform to a perfectionist ideal of "masculinity".[263] If men don't properly conform to the ideal of manliness then they're considered inferior, worthless, and a complete failure by their society.[264] Suppressing emotions, condemning emotions as a sign of utter weakness, and maintaining a stoic demeanor as a form of strength is a

---

3. [262] Freeman, Daniel, and Jason Freeman. "Why are men more likely than women to take their own lives?" *The Guardian*, Guardian News and Media, 21 Jan. 2015, www.theguardian.com/science/2015/jan/21/suicide-gender-men-women-mental-health-nick-clegg.

4. [263] Nietzsche, Friedrich Wilhelm. *On the genealogy of morals: a polemical tract.* Translated by Ian Johnston, PDF, Richer Resources Publications, 2014.

5. [264] Green, Laci. "TOXIC MASCULINITY!" *YouTube*, YouTube, 20 Dec. 2017, www.youtube.com/watch?v=i5juyXjDnJ0.

psychopathic ideal to live towards and a clear form of mental torture.[265][266] Any sign for help, any desire for releasing negative emotions by the natural process of crying, and anything short of being a pillar of strength are situations in which men feel utterly ashamed of themselves because they couldn't measure up to the ideal of a "true man" of society. Under such pitiful notions, taking risky dares that endanger their own life is seen as an optimal form of "manliness" and men can be coerced into doing idiotic actions to prove their "manhood" to other men. Examples of this can be seen throughout different cultures, comments that synonymies strength and the male genitals are examples of this "macho" culture. Drinking alcohol in large portions, driving recklessly, the lack of desire to go to the hospital when physically sick, the need to appear buff, threats of violence as a form of strength, and keeping themselves emotionally distant from their significant other under the pitiful veneer of

6. [265] Nietzsche, Friedrich Wilhelm. *On the genealogy of morals: a polemical tract*. Translated by Ian Johnston, PDF, Richer Resources Publications, 2014.

7. [266] Green, Laci. "TOXIC MASCULINITY!" *YouTube*, YouTube, 20 Dec. 2017, www.youtube.com/watch?v=i5juyXjDnJ0.

"respect" are all examples of the psychopathic behavior of "manliness". For the most part, men are never allowed to convey self-expression, happiness from feeling loved, or other healthy human emotions because of the self-deprecating belief that such gestures of affection are "unmanly" by cultural standards. It is a thought process that makes suicide more desirable than living. It's possibly the reason why men are more likely to commit suicide than women and more attempt violent forms of suicide – a final outcry to "prove" their manhood while embracing death to escape their weariness of life.

Lastly, for this section, I've noticed that men who speak out against feminism usually point to incidents where society is unfair to men; including some of the aforementioned reasons. While feminism does primarily focus on women's issues, many of the most prominent feminist vloggers and intellectuals have also criticized the deplorable social stigmas against men and seek to ameliorate the gender stereotypes against men too.[267] Paradoxically, men who condemn feminism usually reference their own social stigmas as a strange

---

[267] Green, Laci. "TOXIC MASCULINITY!" *YouTube*, YouTube, 20 Dec. 2017, www.youtube.com/watch?v=i5juyXjDnJ0.

"defense" against feminism. Yet, all of the social stigmas the anti-feminists make valid complaints against have originated from the male social identity that they seek to defend against feminism. Feminism isn't being disproven by bringing up such complaints; these men are admitting to have favorable dispositions to feminism while condemning, demonizing, and forming misogynistic rants about the very women who seek to ameliorate these social prejudices against men.

Women's roles: Modesty or Misogyny?

Numbers 31: 7-18. KJV

[7] And they warred against the Midianites, as the LORD commanded Moses; and they slew all the males.

[8] And they slew the kings of Midian, beside the rest of them that were slain; namely, Evi, and Rekem, and Zur, and Hur, and Reba, five kings of Midian: Balaam also the son of Beor they slew with the sword.

[9] And the children of Israel took all the women of Midian captives, and their little ones, and took the spoil of all their cattle, and all their flocks, and all their goods.

[10] And they burnt all their cities wherein they dwelt, and all their goodly castles, with fire.

[11] And they took all the spoil, and all the prey, both of men and of beasts.

[12] And they brought the captives, and the prey, and the spoil, unto Moses, and Eleazar the priest, and unto the congregation of the children of Israel, unto the camp at the plains of Moab, which are by Jordan near Jericho.

[13] And Moses, and Eleazar the priest, and all the princes of the congregation, went forth to meet them without the camp.

[14] And Moses was wroth with the officers of the host, with the captains over thousands, and captains over hundreds, which came from the battle.

[15] And Moses said unto them, Have ye saved all the women alive?

[16] Behold, these caused the children of Israel, through the counsel of Balaam, to commit trespass against the Lord in the matter of Peor, and there was a plague among the congregation of the Lord.

[17] Now therefore kill every male among the little ones, and kill every woman that hath known man by lying with him.

[18] But all the women children, that have not known a man by lying with him, keep alive for yourselves.[268]

Social stigmas against women have gained more attention

throughout the world. The likely reason was the sexism being more

explicit and overt compared to sexist double-standards against men.

In third world countries, this double-standard is plainly undeniable;

women still have barriers against being allowed to read, write, in

certain countries they're barred from the independent right to go

---

8.   [268] "BibleGateway." *Numbers 31:7-18 KJV - - Bible Gateway,* www.biblegateway.com/passage/?search=Numbers 31:7-18&version=KJV.

200

shopping without the presence of a man, and many other crucial issues. In first world countries, there are still issues with the right to an abortion, equal pay, equal promotion in the workforce, equal representation in film and video games, women are still being viewed as promiscuous for choosing what article of clothing to wear, and women who have children out of wedlock are socially stigmatized for their entire life.[269]

However, the majority of these gender stereotypes stem from the belief that women are property to be owned by men; for most ancient religious history, women were seen as spoils of war to be used to make heirs through campaigns of war rape. Ancient religious texts prescribed most of women's gender roles on the basis of being war spoils won by the conquering tribe – the Old Testament is one of the most overt examples and much of the passages are untenable in modern times. The ancient religious beliefs of women being the property of men is the fundamental basis for all of the unequal religious morals imposed upon women. Both culture and society

---

9.   [269] Green, Laci. "WHY I'M A...FEMINIST *Gasp*." *YouTube*, YouTube, 23 Apr. 2014, www.youtube.com/watch?v=UwJRFClybmk.

substitute the reasons to argue that constricting women's actions are for morally good reasons. The premise of the belief system comes from the history of war rape within ancient religious wars; humanity substituted so-called morally good reasons to stay consistent with the ownership of women. Society's attempt at espousing moral reasons for controlling women's bodies are just attempts at trying to stay consistent with the logical fallacy of an appeal to tradition; the appeal to tradition is that women should conduct themselves in certain social manners because that was how it was done before the current generation. They believe this instills good morals in women. Yet, going back further, the commitment to so-called good morals originated from the servitude of women to men as property won through conquest and rape. If you believe the ancient stories of conquering tribes that enacted violence upon others because of God's will then you must realize that the conservative cultural norms imposed upon women came from viewing them as spoils of war.

Several modern-day social stigmas show the war rape mentality. Determining what women should wear so they don't look "inappropriate" in the eyes of men. The belief that women are asking to be raped because they show their bodies in public comes from war rape mentality; that is why there was a tacit assumption that men would have the uncontrollable urge to rape women and why culture constantly views them as objects. Arguments about being proper ladies by remaining "respectful" can still mean obeying the husband as the head of the household within a multitude of religious denominations even in the West and such mentalities often create entire communities where men are allowed to beat their wives with no legal repercussions. Examples of these religious morals still exist in poorer regions of South Carolina in the United States; men are allowed to beat their wives in front of their children, they're known to kill women who flee from abusive households, and police and the communities ignore the violence because of their Christian belief that men are to be heads of the household as decreed in the Bible.[270]

Implementing laws that control their reproductive choices is one of

---

10. [270] "Till death do us part: A Post and Courier Special Report." *Post and Courier*, 19 Aug. 2014, www.postandcourier.com/app/till-death/partone.html.

the most overt examples of inequality imposed upon women.[271]

Parents often have a critical outlook on their daughter's behavior after the age of maturity to the point where they condemn their own children as sluts and whores should their child refuse to conform to gender roles.[272] They probably feel like failed parents should their daughters make independent choices in life about their sexual partners. Women are condemned as sluts and whores for sex out of wedlock. If women have multiple partners then they're condemned as sluts; men who do the same are not and instead men are seen as falling for the "wiles" of women. Both genders are taught to be ashamed of the natural biological process of consensual sex and masturbation by society. Women are viewed as traitorous to some men for showing any amount of their body in public or as "disloyal" because they don't fit the stereotypical standards of staying a virgin until marriage. It comes from the spoils of war mentality; they're

11. [271] Green, Laci. "WHY I'M A...FEMINIST *Gasp*." *YouTube*, YouTube, 23 Apr. 2014, www.youtube.com/watch?v=UwJRFClybmk.

12. [272] Green, Laci. "WHY I'M A...FEMINIST *Gasp*." *YouTube*, YouTube, 23 Apr. 2014, www.youtube.com/watch?v=UwJRFClybmk.

viewed as "used goods" because they can no longer satisfy the expectations of the leering rapist of a warring desert tribe. Furthermore, women who express their sexual liberation are generally assumed to be crying out for help under the patronizing system of religious morality. Euphemisms are made to ignore the intrinsic aspect of women being perceived as spoils of war to justify the discrimination; euphemisms like "respecting the husband", young girls being taught to be "quiet and meek" as a good moral trait, or that women are too emotional to make meaningful choices all come from this ancient cultural history within the major religions. All of this are cultural derivatives of viewing women as spoils of war by following an appeal to tradition and appeal to purity fallacy through substituting the original reason they were imposed upon women with the fallacious reasoning.[273]

---

13. [273] "Appeal to Tradition." *Https://Www.logicallyfallacious.com*, www.logicallyfallacious.com/tools/lp/Bo/LogicalFallacies/44/Appeal-to-Tradition.

Rape Culture and Patriarchy

Unquestioned assumptions about gender norms, based on religious conservative values, are beliefs that can no longer be considered tenable due to their incoherence with gender equality. At the root of the social schism between religious conservatism and liberal social values is the question of whether gender norms are biological or social constructs. In stark contrast to more liberal social perceptions, gender-based human behavior is seen as fixed and unalterable due to religious conservatives perspective on human biology, while liberal schools of thought of human behavior is perceived as grounded in cultural norms that are inculcated from society. These underlying assumptions change how we react to incidents of sexual violence, gender discrimination, and what we perceive to be terrible moral beliefs and practices. While religious conservatism leads people to believe male violence is unalterable and fixed with women always burdened into the receiving end of such treatment, liberal values counter that such beliefs are the causes of violence and perpetuate systems that seek to legitimize gender violence in a self-fulfilling cycle. This liberal criticism is what led many to perceive religious conservative values as hypocritical, but it would be more accurate to say that religious social values are incoherent.

Religious conservative beliefs are ingrained with fixed mindsets and entity theories about gender-based violence and gender-related behavior. That is, they identify and internalize it as unalterable human norms and so don't seek to change societal norms to improve the general welfare of society; they go so far as to work against social changes because of their belief that their religion already provides the best guideline for how humans should behave.[274] Religious conservative values use snap judgments to find simplistic questions and answers to broad problems and this behavior is largely encouraged with religious texts that reinforce entity theories about gender.[275][276] These simplistic assumptions largely contribute to

---

14. [274] Dweck, Carol S. *Mindset: How You Can Fulfill Your Potential.* Random House, 2012.

15. [275] Cialdini, Robert B. Chapter 1: Weapons of Influence (1-16). *Influence: Science and practice.* 4th ed., 21st Century Bks, 2002.

dangerous falsehoods that perpetuate systems of physical, emotional, and sexual abuse that create victims and lead to victim blaming.[277][278] The belief that women must cover-up their bodies so as not to attract male attention, limit their activities at night time to decrease incidents of sexual violence, and learn to follow so-called "modest" behavior to keep from getting attacked by violent men doesn't align with the research on whom rapists target. Conservative religious values simplistic assumptions and answers hold implications of a just-world where the violent atrocity of rape is seen as somehow manageable and controllable on the part of the victim and thus encourages victim blaming when rape occurs.[279] Theresa M. Beiner in a journalistic study for the *Duke Journal of Gender Law and Policy* called *"Sexy Dressing Revisited: Does Target Dress Play a Part in Sexual*

16. [276] Cialdini, Robert B. Chapter 6: Authority (178-200). *Influence: Science and practice*. 4th ed., 21st Century Bks, 2002.

17. [277] Green, Laci. "THE F-WORD." *YouTube*, YouTube, 8 July 2014, www.youtube.com/watch?v=EJPT_U97lNs.

18. [278] Kahneman, Daniel. Chapter 8: How Judgments Happen (89-96). *Thinking, fast and slow*. Farrar, Straus and Giroux, 2015.

19. [279] Grinnell, Renée. "Just-World Hypothesis." *Encyclopedia of Psychology*, 17 July 2016, psychcentral.com/encyclopedia/just-world-hypothesis/.

Harassment Cases?" which researched the impacts of rape victims

attire on legal cases and likelihood of being targeted had surprising

findings to share that upend many conservative social assumptions

about both rapists and their targets. I strongly encourage readers to

read the excerpts related to parts III and IV of her findings below:

III. SOCIAL SCIENCE AND DRESS

"Social science has much to offer in determining the meaning of women's dress and how it might affect sexual harassment cases. A variety of academic disciplines have analyzed women's dress, looking at what it means to both the person wearing the clothing and perceivers of that person as well as its broader social implications. This section discusses several aspects of social science that may help explain why defendants are not using evidence concerning the
provocative nature of the plaintiff's dress to show that the target welcomed the harassment. In doing so, it lays the foundation for the argument, made more explicitly in the next section, that the reason defendants are not seeking to admit evidence of plaintiff's provocative dress in sexual harassment cases as frequently as might be supposed is because provocatively-dressed women may not be the likely targets of sexual harassment.

The section begins by discussing how perceptions of victim dress play a role in perceptions of rape and sexual harassment. In this context it investigates how a woman's dress affects perceptions of that woman in a manner that might have relevance for sexual harassment law. For example, are provocatively dressed women harassed more often, and, more importantly, do people think this is the

case? Do people believe that provocatively dressed women invite harassment? It then looks at what is known about how rapists and, to a lesser extent, sexual harassers, choose their victims in an effort to determine whether common perceptions of the role dress plays in victimization is accurate. From
there it looks at characteristics of both rape and sexual harassment victims to see if, based on who these women are, sexual harassers may be choosing their victims in a manner similar to rapists. It also addresses research about sexual harassers to determine if they share some common characteristics with rapists, which may make some of the research concerning rape applicable to sexual harassment. Finally, it looks for social science explanations for why dress makes a difference in perceptions of who is likely to be harassed. Throughout this section, I rely on social science of rape in situations in which there is little research on sexual harassment. I explain why this is justified at the points in my argument where it becomes relevant.

Underlying rape shield laws is the belief that people, and in particular jurors, mistakenly believe that a women's dress has an impact on whether she will be victimized. This belief is borne out by research on perceptions of women's dress. As one source elucidates:

'Although women with provocative appearances are perceived as sexually attractive and more desirable, they are judged as less intelligent, sincere, trustful, reliable, and less moral than women with non-provocative appearances. . . . Further, . . . "appearance influences judgments of a sender's competence (ability or expertise), even when the task at hand is unrelated to appearance.'"*131*

Clearly, dress influences how people perceive and interact with one another. Yet, assessments of women's attitudes or beliefs based on their dress are not necessarily accurate.

210

For example, while people believe that certain items of clothing signify more liberal sexual attitudes, one study suggests that in reality, few items of clothing actually correlate with such liberal attitudes.132 Thus, generally-held perceptions of sexualized dressing may well be out of sync with any one individual's attitudes and behaviors.

Perhaps most notably, a survey of psychiatrists reported that a three-to-one majority of those responding "said that attire that the male perceives as inviting direct sex attention does, indeed, tend to increase sex crime risk."133 The styles of clothing that psychiatrists thought carried this potential risk included short skirts, see-through dresses, short shorts, and bikinis.134 As they concluded, "[t]he survey replies show that U.S. psychiatrists in large numbers believe that revealing attire is one of the causative or precipitating factors in sex crimes against young females."135 Thus, highly-educated and learned adults believe that how a woman dresses has an impact on whether or not she will be a victim of a sex crime.

The same general findings hold true for dress and sexual harassment. A study involving 200 college students sought to determine whether target dress and gender of a perceiver played a part in determining who was likely to be sexually harassed.136 "The model when wearing provocative clothing was rated significantly higher on likelihood of provoking sexual harassment . . . than when wearing nonprovocative clothing."137 Interestingly, women rated the model dressed provocatively highest on the likelihood of provoking sexual harassment.138 However, men and women did not differ in their assessment of the model wearing nonprovocative clothing.139 This suggests that women are more inclined to believe that provocative dress has an impact on who is harassed. While this study shows women are more inclined to link provocative dress with sexual harassment, it is important to note that both men

211

and women perceive this link. The question remains whether this perception is accurate.

While people perceive dress to have an impact on who is assaulted, studies of rapists suggest that victim attire is not a significant factor. Instead, rapists look for signs of passiveness and submissiveness, which, studies suggest, are more likely to coincide with more body-concealing clothing.140 In a study to test whether males could determine whether women were high or low in passiveness and submissiveness, Richards and her colleagues found that men, using only nonverbal appearance cues, could accurately assess which women were passive and submissive versus those who were dominant and assertive.141 Clothing was one of the key cues: "Those females high in passivity and submissiveness (i.e., those at greatest risk for victimization) wore noticeably more body-concealing clothing (i.e., high necklines, long pants and sleeves,
multiple layers)."142 This suggests that men equate body-concealing clothing with passive and submissive qualities, which are qualities that rapists look for in victims. Thus, those who wore provocative clothes would not be viewed as passive or submissive, and would be less likely to be victims of assault.

Along these lines, research suggests that rape victims are "significantly lower" in "dominance, assertiveness, and social presence."143 While members of the public believe that victims of assault attract such attacks by dressing provocatively,144 attractiveness does not correlate with submissive characteristics in victims.145 Instead, research "specifically revealed a negative relationship between perceptions of attractiveness and traits which could be construed as contributing to a nonverbal appearance of vulnerability."146 Thus:

'Male evaluators perceived attractive females as lower in

submissiveness, uncertainty, simpleness, carelessness and passivity than their less attractive peers. This suggests that conventional definitions of physical attractiveness do not represent visual attributes which enhance a woman's potential for victimization.'147

This seems at odds with studies concerning provocative dress, although no studies have looked directly at provocative dress and submissiveness. Of course, attractiveness and provocative dress are not the same thing. As Glick and his colleagues point out, it can be difficult to alter one's physical attractiveness, "but women can easily emphasize or deemphasize their sexuality through clothing and demeanor."148 Thus, dressing sexy or provocatively is a choice that may or
may not lead to a woman being perceived as attractive. Still, women who dress provocatively may be exhibiting a degree of confidence that does not suggest submissiveness. These women would be less likely to be victims of sexual assault or harassment, because potential abusers would not perceive them as passive or submissive.

No studies were readily available that explained how sexual harassers target their victims. However, there is information about who is more likely to be targeted for sexual harassment. Interestingly, it parallels what is known about rape victims: "Young and single women tend to be the targets of sexual harassment."149 However, sexual harassment can happen to any women, and, studies show, once other factors are considered (such as workplace characteristics and the form the sexual harassment takes), the impact of age and marital status on who is harassed lessens considerably.150 Youth and being single are factors related to power. As one researcher observed, "[d]ifferences in age, marital status, and education reinforce gender differences in power and status in society."151 Thus, because sexual harassment is about power, differences in these power-related statuses are likely to correlate with who is sexually harassed.

This parallels research on rape victims. While, like sexual harassment, any woman can be a rape victim, "studies have shown that the rape victim is more likely to be a single, white or black young female, from a lower social working class. Further 'women who are most vulnerable to rape exhibit lower levels of psychosocial effectiveness' and tend to have passive or submissive personalities prior to the assaults."152

Thus, it appears that victims of rape and victims of sexual harassment share some common characteristics. Yet, much of the research discussed above involves how rapists choose their victims—not how sexual harassers choose their targets. Thus, it may not be directly applicable to sexual harassment. However, research also suggests that perpetrators of more serious sexual harassment are on a continuum with rapists.153 Research on rapists might be likewise helpful in determining how sexual harassers choose their targets. Sexual harassers, like rapists, may pick victims who are vulnerable and submissive. Research on men who are likely to sexually harass suggests that this leap is logical.

Psychologist John Pryor was one of the first to study characteristics of men who sexually harass. He developed a scale to determine the propensity of men to sexually harass.154 His sexual harassment research is based, in part, on the research of those who study rape. As he explains, "[m]any researchers believe rape and severe forms of sexual harassment are conceptually similar forms of behavior."155 Researchers see rape as on a continuum of "maleaggressive/female-passive" interactions that involve differing levels of coercion and sexual intimacy.156 This led Pryor to opine that rapists and sexual harassers might have some characteristics in common. As a result, he set out to study characteristics of sexual harassers to see if

214

this was true.

Pryor examined those who would be inclined to engage in sexual exploitation, essentially what amounts to quid pro quo harassment. Pryor used various other scales, including those that measured certain attitudes about sex roles and beliefs, attitudes towards feminism, likelihood to rape, and one that measured empathy.157 What he found was a strong relationship between the likelihood-to-sexually-harass scale (LSH) and adversary sexual beliefs and rapemyth acceptance.158 Weaker relationships were found for sex-role stereotyping and acceptance of interpersonal violence.159 Tellingly, "[t]he single best predictor of LSH was Malamuth's (1981) LR [likelihood-to-rape] scale. This result . . . supports [another researcher's] contention that rape and severe forms of sexual harassment represent different degrees of coercive sexual conduct."160 Interestingly, men who scored higher on the LSH scale also had a harder time understanding the perspective of others.161 As Pryor explained, "[t]he profile of a person who is likely to initiate severe sexually harassing behavior that emerges from the initial study is one that emphasizes sexual and social male dominance."162

This scale has proven useful after further study. As Pryor and Stoller point out, "the LSH scale measures a readiness to use social power for sexually exploitative purposes. This suggests that social dominance and male sexuality may be closely aligned concepts in the minds of high-LSH men."163 In a subsequent study, they found that dominance was the best predictor of LSH in men. As they explained, "[t]his finding seems to buttress the argument that dominance and sexuality are integrally related for high-LSH men."164 Thus, it seems appropriate to opine that sexual harassers might choose their targets in a manner similar to that of rapists. These two groups of perpetrators share common characteristics. Further, sexual harassment by high LSH men appears to be triggered by power imbalances—the kind of imbalances that might well be triggered by target submissiveness.

This conclusion is inconsistent with the common belief that how a woman dresses has an impact on whether she will be sexually harassed or sexually assaulted. Why then, do many people, including psychiatrists, assume that dress plays some part in who is a victim of sexual assaults? In particular, why do women believe this? Social scientists believe this is the result of the "just world hypothesis." As Melvin Lerner explained,

'for their own security, if for no other reason, people want to believe they live in a just world where people get what they deserve. One way of accomplishing this is by . . . persuading himself that the victim deserved to suffer, after all. The assumption here is that attaching responsibility to behavior provides us with the greater security—we can do something to avoid such a fate.'165

Thus, in the context of sexual harassment, this explains why women, more than men, are inclined to believe that provocative dress has an impact on who is sexually harassed. Women attribute the harassment to something the victim has done, such as wearing provocative clothing, as a way to understand how it could happen to someone else and not to them. Thus, blaming the victim, for example, by believing she provoked the behavior by her dress, makes other women believe that dressing differently (i.e., more "appropriately") will prevent it from happening to them.166

This is closely related to another theory known as "harm avoidance." Women blame victims as a way to exercise control over their lives and to continue to believe that bad things, including sexual harassment and sexual assaults, will not happen to them.167 Thus, by viewing provocative dress as a factor in sexual harassment, women believe that they can avoid sexual harassment simply by not dressing provocatively. Both of these theories provide explanations as to why women, in particular, may think that harassment or sexual assault is provoked by victim dress.

Thus, how people commonly perceive the role of a target's dress in sexual harassment appears to be out of sync with how sexual harassers may choose their targets. This leads to a possible explanation as to why defendants are not using target dress to prove unwelcomeness."[280]

IV. IMPLICATIONS OF DRESS FOR SEXUAL HARASSMENT LAW

"The social science described above suggests some potential explanations as to why defendants do not regularly raise the issue of target dress to rebut unwelcomeness in sexual harassment cases. Given the purported recent increase in provocative dress by women168 and the lack of a solid legal standard against its admission, one would expect to see defendants using arguments and evidence about target dress to prove welcomeness—or at least, to *dis*-prove *un*welcomeness. Yet, this practice appears uncommon. How does one account for this? Earlier in this article I suggested several potential explanations. First, it could be that defendants are not raising it because they believe either that they will not

---

20. [280] BEINER, THERESA M. III. SOCIAL SCIENCE AND DRESS (143-148). "SEXY DRESSING REVISITED: DOES TARGET DRESS PLAY A PART IN SEXUAL HARASSMENT CASES? ." *Duke University School of Law*, Duke Journal of Gender Law & Policy, 2007, scholarship.law.duke.edu/cgi/viewcontent.cgi?&article=1109&context=djg lp.

be successful in having the evidence admitted under Rule 412 or that the factfinder will be in some way offended by such attempts. Essentially, the tactic might backfire on the defendant. Second, it is possible that women who wear provocative clothing to work do not mind the attention that they receive from it and therefore are not bringing sexual harassment claims. Third, it is possible that victim dress does not have an impact on who is sexually harassed. Legal feminists have long argued that sexual harassment is about power. With this in mind, the work of social scientists suggests that potential harassers might choose their targets using criteria other than dress.

Legal and social science scholars have proposed a number of theories suggesting why and how sexual harassment occurs. The foremost legal scholar on this issue, Catharine MacKinnon, posited early on that sexual harassment is about power differences between men and women. Sexual harassment is a tool used to perpetuate hierarchy, the principal way in which men maintain their dominance in American society.169 As several psychology researchers described the theory,

'[a]ccording to this model, male dominance is maintained by cultural patterns of male-female interaction as well as by economic and political superordinancy. Society rewards males for aggressive and domineering sexual behaviors and females for passivity and acquiescence. . . . [T]he function of sexual harassment is to manage ongoing male-female interactions according to accepted sex status norms, and to maintain male dominance occupationally and therefore economically, by intimidating, discouraging, or precipitating removal of women from work.'170

This theory fits well with what is known about men who sexually harass. These men are influenced by dominance—power—in their relationships with women. Thus, this

218

provides an explanation of why women who are provocatively dressed might not be bringing sexual harassment cases: They are not good potential targets for harassers. If, as studies of rapists suggest, harassers look for more passive or submissive women, women who are provocatively dressed may appear more confident and are therefore less likely to be considered appropriate targets by potential harassers. Indeed, the cases involving requests that women dress more professionally or tone down their sexy attire suggest that people are generally uncomfortable with women who dress provocatively in the workplace. The power dynamic involved in telling women to dress less provocatively (essentially trying to control their attire) is also interesting. It suggests that there is power in dressing provocatively, and that employers are uncomfortable by such assertions of this power by women.171

I am aware that I am extrapolating at least in part from research on rapists for this argument. This is one area that requires further study by social scientists to determine whether sexual harassers are picking their targets much like rapists pick their victims—based on indications of passivity and submissiveness. At this point, this theory is somewhat speculative—rapists and sexual harassers share some common characteristics, and victims of rape and sexual harassment also share several common characteristics. To the extent that there is incomplete research on sexual harassers, this essay serves as a call to social scientists who study sexual harassment to do further scholarship on how sexual harassers choose their targets.

There is another problem with this potential explanation. Just because a woman is dressed provocatively does not mean that she is necessarily confident and therefore less likely to be submissive. It could well be that her lack of confidence is what induces her to dress provocatively, in an attempt to draw what she considers to be positive attention to herself. Perhaps there is a class of cases that never make it to court because the women involved do not find the attention their attire garners harassing. Indeed, they may enjoy the attention. Further, to the extent that the attention is considered complimentary (i.e., it is not derogatory or otherwise demeaning), it may not be objectionable by these women.

Other sexual harassment theorists posit that sexual harassment is a result of an interaction between people and workplace characteristics and situations.172 Workplace environments in which sexualized images, comments, and behavior toward women are tolerated are more likely to be those in which women are sexually harassed.173 This theory, however, is not inconsistent with the power/dominance model. In workplaces with such atmospheres, women are placed in less powerful positions: They are essentially deemed sex objects. It is little wonder that sexual harassment thrives in such environments, given the little organizational power afforded to women.

This also might explain the one set of cases where provocatively dressed women are commonly harassed: the Hooters cases. Studies show that men high in LSH are aware of situational constraints on their behavior.174 Thus, in an environment like Hooters, where the Hooters Girl's "predominant function is to provide vicarious sexual recreation, to titillate, entice, and arouse male customers' fantasies,"175 men who are likely to sexually harass will consider the Hooters' business plan to permit (perhaps even encourage) such harassment. Thus, while provocative dress might signal confidence in an office setting, at Hooters, workplace norms encourage men who are so inclined to harass.

What about the women who complain about men making comments about their attire as part of their sexual harassment allegations? It is not clear whether these women were dressed in a provocative manner or not.

Certainly, in some cases they were not. For example, in
Conley v. City of Lincoln City, the plaintiff
was in her police uniform.176 In addition, employers in
these cases (aside for rare exceptions such as the lingerie
case177) did not argue that something about the plaintiff's
attire "caused" the plaintiff to be harassed. Yet, clearly
inappropriate comments—including those that are sexually
demeaning—about workplace dress offend women. They
are a weapon in the arsenal of harassing behaviors that
affect women's employment. Some of these comments
clearly would undermine a woman's workplace authority,
because the comments are demeaning and thereby
undermine the plaintiff's power and authority in the
workplace. Even in the case involving the police chief,
commenting, although apparently in a complimentary
fashion, about her attire could cast her as something to
look at rather than someone who leads the police force.
One could imagine how these comments might have
affected her ability to lead and why she included them in
her complaint. Thus, comments about dress are used to
undermine the workplace authority of women and should
be included in the appropriate case as part of a plaintiff's
sexual harassment allegations."[281]

It may come with shock and a sense of unease for those with

conservative religious values that women with provocative attire,

---

21. [281] BEINER, THERESA M. IV. IMPLICATIONS OF DRESS FOR
SEXUAL HARASSMENT LAW (148-151). "SEXY DRESSING
REVISITED: DOES TARGET DRESS PLAY A PART IN SEXUAL
HARASSMENT CASES? ." *Duke University School of Law*, Duke Journal
of Gender Law & Policy, 2007,
scholarship.law.duke.edu/cgi/viewcontent.cgi?&article=1109&context=djg
lp.

generally expressing a show of confidence, are far less likely to be targets of rapists and that women who cover their bodies are the most likely to be attacked and raped. This is because the underlying assumptions of what rape constitutes in the view of religious conservatism is wrong and the assumptions have corrosive effects on rape victims who are subjected to systems of abuse. By assuming that women must be kept meek and obedient, fully clothed to avoid male attention, and have their ability to socialize curtailed so that they'll be safe is precisely the sort of behavior that rapists look for to get away with rape. By being socially conditioned to be submissive, they're easier prey for people with coercive intentions and less likely to speak out or push back when forced into an uncomfortable situation. By limiting their social outings and social relationships, they're less likely to have a strong social support group that they can go to for help when confronted with coercive people. By teaching young women that covering-up avoids rape, religious conservatism is instilling a dangerous illusion of immunity and an ignorance towards what people can and cannot control in their daily lives.[282] The worst aspect of these religiously motivated beliefs is the process of shaming, ridicule, and societal disdain that may force a rape victim to relive the trauma of the sexual violence done to them and they may inculcate the belief that somehow they were deserving of being raped because of how their community treats them with derision or the fear that their community will treat them with such hostility should they come forward. As a direct result of a religious upbringing and a socially conservative community, a rape victim may be too fearful to come forward about what happened to them. This self-reinforcing cycle of systematic sexual abuse as a result of conservative social values is what is known as rape culture and religious norms are an intrinsic component of this belief system. This systematic social ill is a focal component of what feminists refer to as the patriarchy.

While the patriarchal structures of religiously conservative societies create nefariously unequal treatment towards women and

---

22. [282] Grinnell, Renée. "Just-World Hypothesis." *Encyclopedia of Psychology*, 17 July 2016, psychcentral.com/encyclopedia/just-world-hypothesis/.

such structures comprise of rape culture, these very same gender stereotypes are just as harmful to men. A disgusting and asinine view perpetuated by religious conservative values is that it is simply expected that men will rape women under the belief that men can't control themselves with ignorant adages such as "boys will be boys" or implications that it's just expected that rape will happen when men and women are together in any social setting. In the purview of sexual violence against women, the implicit argument made when a person questions what a woman was wearing, what a woman was drinking, or what she was doing when outside late at night without questioning a male rapist's behavior is to assume that it's just expected that men will rape women. Any man who makes these arguments implicate themselves and heavily imply that they would also commit rape crimes against rape victims in the context of how each specific case of sexual violence happened, because to them it's somehow normal that men would rape women or desire to rape women; they normalize the idea that women should never feel safe around any man or they'll be punished for wanting to live equally. Obviously, the majority of men wouldn't do such a despicable act, what it does indicate is the normalization of gender stereotypes without any self-critique on just what sort of arguments people are espousing by thoughtlessly following religious traditions.[283]

Gender stereotypes about men pressure them into conforming to belief systems that require them to be emotionless under the guise that they're invulnerable. Any expression of vulnerability is an admittance of weakness and treated with derision in typical patriarchal societies. This illusion of emotional immunity being a cornerstone of maleness leads to dire consequences. Physical violence between men is often seen as more acceptable when men do it due to the culturally ingrained and wrong social stereotype that testosterone causes men to be prone to violence when studies indicate that it is more nuanced than that.[284] Male aggressive behavior with respect to

23. [283] Cialdini, Robert B. Chapter 6: Authority (178-200). *Influence: Science and practice*. 4th ed., 21st Century Bks, 2002.
24. [284] Mims, Christopher. "Strange but True: Testosterone Alone Does Not Cause Violence." *Scientific American*, 5 July 2007, www.scientificamerican.com/article/strange-but-true-testosterone-alone-doesnt-cause-violence/.

testosterone is concomitant with elevating one's status, testosterone

can lead to generosity such as donating to charities, and aggressive

people in both genders have higher testosterone levels than the

average.[285][286][287] Male questions, worries, or insecurities about the act

of sex can be treated as points of mockery and derision because it's

assumed that men must intrinsically desire sex without any curiosity

or concern for further information or informed decision-making on

their part. The idea of masculine toughness can preclude any freedom

for vulnerability or to express one's emotions in a peaceful manner;

crying is seen as a sign of weakness, backing away from

confrontation is seen as a sign of being a lesser man, and generally

expressing any discomfort or criticism is seen as an admittance of

25. [285] Batrinos, Menelaos L. "Testosterone and Aggressive Behavior in Man." *International Journal of Endocrinology and Metabolism*, NCBI, 2012, www.ncbi.nlm.nih.gov/pmc/articles/PMC3693622/.

26. [286] Healy, Melissa. "In addition to fueling aggression, testosterone can also make men more generous, study says." *Los Angeles Times*, Los Angeles Times, 26 Sept. 2016, www.latimes.com/science/sciencenow/la-sci-sn-testosterone-behavior-men-20160926-snap-story.html.

27. [287] Mims, Christopher. "Strange but True: Testosterone Alone Does Not Cause Violence." *Scientific American*, 5 July 2007, www.scientificamerican.com/article/strange-but-true-testosterone-alone-doesnt-cause-violence/.

defeat or weakness and treated with derision. Thus, men never learn to deal with personal insecurities in a adequate or healthy manner because emotional growth is inhibited by conservative norms about male behavior. What feminists critique as male entitlement is more akin to male insecurity being forced upon women. Within the conservative religious paradigm, wives are expected to avoid talking to or interacting with strangers who are men for fear they'll cheat on their husbands, women are expected to stay at home to raise children without much social contact outside the home, and they're expected to "respect" the husband by obedience to the male authority of the household.[288] These patriarchal social conditions of control are both oppressive to women and a result of appeasing male insecurities instead of trusting women and treating them equally.

The gender stereotype of men under religious conservatism can lead to pathological social catastrophes in war time. Whilst religious conservatism tacitly treats women as spoils of war from war

28. [288] Cialdini, Robert B. Chapter 6: Authority (178-200). *Influence: Science and practice.* 4th ed., 21st Century Bks, 2002.

rape through its traditionalist mindset without any self-criticism or scrutiny, it treats male victims of war rape even worse; it's considered impossible within religious conservatism for men to be victims of rape. Their emotional and physical pain is treated with mockery, derision, and hate by patriarchal religious customs. Journalist Will Storr wrote an article for *The Guardian* titled *The Rape of Men: The Darkest Secret of War* in which he tackles the lack of compassion, sensitivity, and effort put into helping male victims of war rape specifically due to patriarchal religious customs that perpetuate rape culture from religiously conservative societies:

Of all the secrets of war, there is one that is so well kept that it exists mostly as a rumour. It is usually denied by the perpetrator and his victim. Governments, aid agencies and human rights defenders at the UN barely acknowledge its possibility. Yet every now and then someone gathers the courage to tell of it. This is just what happened on an ordinary afternoon in the office of a kind and careful counsellor in Kampala, Uganda. For four years Eunice Owiny had been employed by Makerere University's Refugee Law Project (RLP) to help displaced people from all over Africa work through their traumas. This particular case, though, was a puzzle. A female client was having marital difficulties. "My husband can't have sex," she complained. "He feels very bad about this. I'm sure there's something he's keeping from me."

Owiny invited the husband in. For a while they got nowhere. Then Owiny asked the wife to leave. The man then murmured cryptically: "It happened to me." Owiny frowned. He reached into his pocket and pulled out an old sanitary pad. "Mama Eunice," he said. "I am in pain. I have to use this."

Laying the pus-covered pad on the desk in front of him, he gave up his secret. During his escape from the civil war in neighbouring Congo, he had been separated from his wife and taken by rebels. His captors raped him, three times a day, every day for three years. And he wasn't the only one. He watched as man after man was taken and raped. The wounds of one were so grievous that he died in the cell in front of him.

"That was hard for me to take," Owiny tells me today. "There are certain things you just don't believe can happen to a man, you get me? But I know now that sexual violence against men is a huge problem. Everybody has heard the women's stories. But nobody has heard the men's."

It's not just in East Africa that these stories remain unheard. One of the few academics to have looked into the issue in any detail is Lara Stemple, of the University of California's Health and Human Rights Law Project. Her study *Male Rape and Human Rights* notes incidents of male sexual violence as a weapon of wartime or political aggression in countries such as Chile, Greece, Croatia, Iran, Kuwait, the former Soviet Union and the former Yugoslavia. Twenty-one per cent of Sri Lankan males who were seen at a London torture treatment centre reported sexual abuse while in detention. In El Salvador, 76% of male political prisoners surveyed in the 1980s described at least one incidence of sexual torture. A study of 6,000 concentration-camp inmates in Sarajevo found that 80% of men reported having been raped.

I've come to Kampala to hear the stories of the few brave men who have agreed to speak to me: a rare opportunity to find out about a controversial and deeply taboo issue. In Uganda, survivors are at risk of arrest by police, as they are likely to assume that they're gay – a crime in this country and in 38 of the 53 African nations. They will probably be ostracised by friends, rejected by family and turned away by the UN and the myriad international NGOs that are equipped, trained and ready to help women. They are wounded, isolated and in danger. In the words of Owiny: "They are despised."

But they are willing to talk, thanks largely to the RLP's British director, Dr Chris Dolan. Dolan first heard of wartime sexual violence against men in the late 1990s while researching his PhD in northern Uganda, and he sensed that the problem might be dramatically underestimated. Keen to gain a fuller grasp of its depth and nature, he put up posters throughout Kampala in June 2009 announcing a "workshop" on the issue in a local school. On the day, 150 men arrived. In a burst of candour, one attendee admitted: "It's happened to all of us here." It soon became known among Uganda's 200,000-strong refugee population that the RLP were helping men who had been raped during conflict. Slowly, more victims began to come forward.

I meet Jean Paul on the hot, dusty roof of the RLP's HQ in Old Kampala. He wears a scarlet high-buttoned shirt and holds himself with his neck lowered, his eyes cast towards the ground, as if in apology for his impressive height. He has a prominent upper lip that shakes continually – a nervous condition that makes him appear as if he's on the verge of tears.

Jean Paul was at university in Congo, studying electronic engineering, when his father – a wealthy businessman – was accused by the army of aiding the enemy and shot dead. Jean Paul fled in January 2009, only to be abducted by rebels. Along with six other men and six women he was marched to a forest in the Virunga National Park.

Later that day, the rebels and their prisoners met up with their cohorts who were camped out in the woods. Small camp fires could be seen here and there between the shadowy ranks of trees. While the women were sent off to prepare food and coffee, 12 armed fighters surrounded the men. From his place on the ground, Jean Paul looked up to see the commander leaning over them. In his 50s, he was bald, fat and in military uniform. He wore a red bandana around his neck and had strings of leaves tied around his elbows.

"You are all spies," the commander said. "I will show you how we punish spies." He pointed to Jean Paul. "Remove your clothes and take a position like a Muslim man."

Jean Paul thought he was joking. He shook his head and said: "I cannot do these things."

The commander called a rebel over. Jean Paul could see that he was only about nine years old. He was told, "Beat this man and remove this clothes." The boy attacked him with his gun butt. Eventually, Jean Paul begged: "Okay, okay. I will take off my clothes." Once naked, two rebels held him in a kneeling position with his head pushed towards the earth.

At this point, Jean Paul breaks off. The shaking in his lip more pronounced than ever, he lowers his head a little further and says: "I am sorry for the things I am going to say now." The commander put his left hand on the back of his skull and used his right to beat him on the backside "like a horse". Singing a witch doctor song, and with everybody watching, the commander then began. The moment he started, Jean Paul vomited.

Eleven rebels waited in a queue and raped Jean Paul in turn. When he was too exhausted to hold himself up, the next attacker would wrap his arm under Jean Paul's hips and lift him by the stomach. He bled freely: "Many, many, many bleeding," he says, "I could feel it like water." Each of the male prisoners was raped 11 times that night and every night that followed.

On the ninth day, they were looking for firewood when Jean Paul spotted a huge tree with roots that formed a small grotto of shadows. Seizing his moment, he crawled in and watched, trembling, as the rebel guards searched for him. After five hours of watching their feet as they hunted for him, he listened as they came up with a plan: they would let off a round of gunfire and tell the commander that Jean Paul had been killed. Eventually he emerged, weak from his ordeal and his diet of only two bananas per day during his captivity. Dressed only in his underpants, he crawled through the undergrowth "slowly, slowly, slowly, slowly, like a snake" back into town.

Today, despite his hospital treatment, Jean Paul still bleeds when he walks. Like many victims, the wounds are such that he's supposed to restrict his diet to soft foods such as bananas, which are expensive, and Jean Paul can only afford maize and millet. His brother keeps asking what's wrong with him. "I don't want to tell him," says Jean Paul. "I fear he will say: 'Now, my brother is not a man.'"

It is for this reason that both perpetrator and victim enter a conspiracy of silence and why male survivors often find, once their story is discovered, that they lose the support and comfort of those around them. In the patriarchal societies found in many developing countries, gender roles are strictly defined.

"In Africa no man is allowed to be vulnerable," says RLP's gender officer Salome Atim. "You have to be masculine, strong. You should never break down or cry. A man must be a leader and provide for the whole family. When he fails to reach that set standard, society perceives that there is something wrong."

Often, she says, wives who discover their husbands have been raped decide to leave them. "They ask me: 'So now how am I going to live with him? As what? Is this still a husband? Is it a wife?' They ask, 'If he can be raped, who is protecting me?' There's one family I have been working closely with in which the husband has been raped twice. When his wife discovered this, she went home, packed her belongings, picked up their child and left. Of course that brought down this man's heart."

Back at RLP I'm told about the other ways in which their clients have been made to suffer. Men aren't simply raped, they are forced to penetrate holes in banana trees that run with acidic sap, to sit with their genitals over a fire, to drag rocks tied to their penis, to give oral sex to queues of soldiers, to be penetrated with screwdrivers and sticks. Atim has now seen so many male survivors that, frequently, she can spot them the moment they sit down. "They tend to lean forward and will often sit on one buttock," she tells me. "When they cough, they grab their lower regions. At times, they will stand up and there's blood on the chair. And they often have some kind of smell."

Because there has been so little research into the rape of men during war, it's not possible to say with any certainty why it happens or even how common it is – although a rare 2010 survey, published in the *Journal of the American Medical Association*, found that 22% of men and 30% of women in Eastern Congo reported conflict-related sexual violence. As for Atim, she says: "Our staff are overwhelmed by the cases we've got, but in terms of actual numbers? This is the tip of the iceberg."

Later on I speak with Dr Angella Ntinda, who treats referrals from the RLP. She tells me: "Eight out of 10 patients from RLP will be talking about some sort of sexual abuse."

"Eight out of 10 men?" I clarify.

"No. Men *and* women," she says.

"What about men?"

"I think all the men."

I am aghast.

"*All* of them?" I say.

"Yes," she says. "All the men."

The research by Lara Stemple at the University of California doesn't only show that male sexual violence is a component of wars all over the world, it also suggests that international aid organisations are failing male victims. Her study cites a review of 4,076 NGOs that have addressed wartime sexual violence. Only 3% of them mentioned the experience of men in their literature. "Typically," Stemple says, "as a passing reference.[289]

Storr discusses the underreporting with Chris Dolan, the Director of the Refugee Law Project, which works in partnership with Christian Aid in highlighting these social issues:

> Stemple's findings on the failure of aid agencies is no surprise to Dolan. "The organisations working on sexual and gender-based violence don't talk about it," he says. "It's systematically silenced. If you're very, very lucky they'll give it a tangential mention at the end of a report. You might get five seconds of: 'Oh and men can also be the victims of sexual violence.' But there's no data, no discussion."
>
> As part of an attempt to correct this, the RLP produced a documentary in 2010 called *Gender Against Men.* When it was screened, Dolan says that attempts were made to stop him. "Were these attempts by people in well-known, international aid agencies?" I ask.
>
> "Yes," he replies. "There's a fear among them that this is a zero-sum game; that there's a pre-defined cake and if you start talking about men, you're going to somehow eat a chunk of this cake that's taken them a long time to bake." Dolan points to a November 2006 UN report that followed an international conference on sexual violence in this area of East Africa.
>
> "I know for a fact that the people behind the report insisted the definition of rape be restricted to women," he says, adding that one of the RLP's donors, Dutch Oxfam, refused to provide any more funding unless he'd promise that 70% of his client base was female. He also recalls a man whose case was "particularly bad" and was referred to the UN's refugee

---

29. [289] Storr, Will. "The rape of men: the darkest secret of war." *The Observer*, Guardian News and Media, 16 July 2011, www.theguardian.com/society/2011/jul/17/the-rape-of-men.

agency, the UNHCR. "They told him: 'We have a programme for vulnerable women, but not men.'"

It reminds me of a scene described by Eunice Owiny: "There is a married couple," she said. "The man has been raped, the woman has been raped. Disclosure is easy for the woman. She gets the medical treatment, she gets the attention, she's supported by so many organisations. But the man is inside, dying."

"In a nutshell, that's exactly what happens," Dolan agrees. "Part of the activism around women's rights is: 'Let's prove that women are as good as men.' But the other side is you should look at the fact that men can be weak and vulnerable."

Margot Wallström, the UN special representative of the secretary-general for sexual violence in conflict, insists in a statement that the UNHCR extends its services to refugees of both genders. But she concedes that the "great stigma" men face suggests that the real number of survivors is higher than that reported. Wallström says the focus remains on women because they are "overwhelmingly" the victims. Nevertheless, she adds, "we do know of many cases of men and boys being raped."

But when I contact Stemple by email, she describes a "constant drum beat that women are *the* rape victims" and a milieu in which men are treated as a "monolithic perpetrator class".

"International human rights law leaves out men in nearly all instruments designed to address sexual violence," she continues. "The UN Security Council Resolution 1325 in 2000 treats wartime sexual violence as something that only impacts on women and girls… Secretary of State Hillary Clinton recently announced $44m to implement this resolution. Because of its entirely exclusive focus on female victims, it seems unlikely that any of these new funds will reach the thousands of men and boys who suffer from this kind of abuse. Ignoring male rape not only neglects men, it also harms women by reinforcing a viewpoint that equates 'female' with 'victim', thus hampering our ability to see women as strong and empowered. In the same way, silence about male victims reinforces unhealthy expectations about men and their supposed invulnerability."

Considering Dolan's finding that "female rape is significantly underreported and male rape almost never", I ask Stemple if, following her research, she believes it might be a hitherto unimagined part of all wars.

"No one knows, but I do think it's safe to say that it's likely that it's been a part of many wars throughout history and that taboo has played a part in the silence."

As I leave Uganda, there's a detail of a story that I can't forget. Before receiving help from the RLP, one man went to see his local doctor. He told him he had been raped four times, that he was injured and depressed and his wife had threatened to leave him. The doctor gave him a Panadol.[290]

Overall, simplistic religious gender norms are unhealthy, they make people less safe in society, they fail to help rape victims who suffer needlessly from worthless gender expectations inculcated by religious conservatism, they act as an impediment towards strong social support for rape victims when they need it most, they blame the victims for the sexual violence they suffer, and they fail to make any coherent or logical sense. How can religious conservatism tout superior morality to liberal social values, while forcing women into a marginalized social status under the implication that all men are prone to rape them? These fixed mindsets and the structural systems of abuse that they propagate can only be diminished and overcome through challenging the foundational assumptions of the simplistic

---

30. [290] Storr, Will. "The rape of men: the darkest secret of war." *The Observer*, Guardian News and Media, 16 July 2011, www.theguardian.com/society/2011/jul/17/the-rape-of-men.

gender binary. The only way to challenge it is by motivating people to value consent and social equality among men and women over abusive systems of unequal social power as encouraged by religious conservatism. Sex-positive feminism that repudiates the shaming of rape victims, pointing out gender discrimination and speaking out on our stories of societal gender bias, statistical analysis of gender equality to measure real progress, and recognizing the pathologies of religious conservatism can offer some assistance to achieve a more equal world.[291]

Female Genital Mutilation

Female circumcision is a widespread practice throughout sub-Saharan Africa and has a long history that predates the creation of the Abrahamic faiths. Despite the typical assumptions made by the West about the practice existing because of male discrimination against women, the practice of this genital mutilation of female babies is most staunchly defended by the elderly women who were forced to

31. [291] Green, Laci. "THE F-WORD." *YouTube*, YouTube, 8 July 2014, www.youtube.com/watch?v=EJPT_U97lNs.

undergo female genital mutilation themselves as babies. It seems to exist because of the special tribal meaning that sub-Saharan Africa placed upon female circumcision from religious traditions predating the conversion to the Abrahamic faiths but exists in the Shafi'i school of Islam in modern times too.[292] Author Hanny Lightfoot-Klein, who worked as a schoolteacher in sub-Saharan Africa and authored the book "Prisoners of Ritual: An Odyssey into female genital circumcision in Africa" elaborates for the NOCIRC symposium (National Organization of Circumcision Resource Center) about the results of her interviews throughout sub-Saharan Africa. She wrote the following:

> Contrary to all my expectations, I discovered that this ancient custom as adhered to and defended most resolutely not by men, but by its survivors, the women elders. It was these women that insisted most vehemently on its perpetuation and it was they who also wielded the knife.
>
> Among the elite, the mutilation was often plotted by "the grandmothers," and carried out at the first unguarded moment that presented itself, in spite of all efforts that the child's educated parents had exerted in order to prevent it.

---

32. [292] "Appeal to Tradition." *Https://Www.logicallyfallacious.com*, www.logicallyfallacious.com/tools/lp/Bo/LogicalFallacies/44/Appeal-to-Tradition.

To nearly all the population, male and female alike, the mere idea that a girl should not be "circumcised" was altogether unthinkable. Not only would such a girl find no one who would marry her, but it was generally believed that all sorts of evils in respect to her sexual behavior, her health, and even more importantly in these cultures, the health of her husband and babies, would inevitably follow.

Eighty-seven percent of men and 83 percent of women voiced their unqualified approval of the practice, according to Dareer's extensive statistical study in Sudan. Taking into consideration that these mutilations are illegal under current Sudanese law, it is almost inevitable that the true approval rate is far closer to 100 percent for both men and women.

I learned that only a tiny handful of the most highly educated Africans had any notion whatsoever that in most of the world "female circumcision" was not practiced at all. Certainly, in the part of sub-Saharan East Africa where I researched the topic most intensively, a vulva left in its natural state stigmatized the woman as a slave, a prostitute, an outcast, an unclean being unworthy of the honor of continuing a respected family lineage.

Among the many people in all walks of life that I interviewed on the subject of female genital mutilation in Sudan, the epicenter of the most extreme excisions and infibulations, there was a young veterinarian who related the following to me:

"It had simply never occurred to me that there was anything wrong with the practice. Nor had this apparently ever occurred to any of my contemporaries, with whom I had at one time or another discussed it. It was only when I studied at a European university and saw how much less complicated things were for women there, that I finally understood how terrible a thing it is."[293]

It may come as a surprise that the very women who were forced into dreadful operations are the staunchest advocates of female babies undergoing genital mutilation but it becomes clearer when

---

33. [293] Lightfoot-Klein, Hanny . *National Organization of Circumcision Resource Centers*, NOCIRC, Mar. 1994, www.nocirc.org/symposia/third/hanny3.html.

understanding the cultural boundaries that exist in sub-Saharan Africa. The people of those regions have sacred beliefs pertaining to female circumcision that are similar to a rite of passage among their community; social proof – following other people in the broad public as a sign of approval that you're conducting the right actions – is one of the core reasons for the prevalence of female circumcision, women who have undergone circumcision often appeal to tradition to justify circumcising babies, they may feel that because they underwent a symbolic concession that it is only appropriate that the younger babies undergo the concession too as a form of collective reciprocity and "equality", and scientific studies have shown, in the case of such tribal practices, fraternity hazing ceremonies, and other such rites of passage, that the more effort imposed through the ritual then the more committed the people are to the specific practice.[294][295]

---

34. [294] Cialdini, Robert B. Chapter 3: Commitment and Consistency (52-95) and Chapter 4: Social Proof (98-140). *Influence: Science and practice*. 4th ed., 21st Century Bks, 2002.

35. [295] "Appeal to Tradition." *Https://Www.logicallyfallacious.com*, www.logicallyfallacious.com/tools/lp/Bo/LogicalFallacies/44/Appeal-to-Tradition.

Generally speaking, people who go through a great deal of effort to obtain something will value it higher.[296] The actual value of what is gained doesn't matter; people's perception of the perceived gain is ranked higher should they struggle to obtain the gain regardless of how worthless the gain actually is.[297] Thus a tribal practice such as female circumcision that is generally accepted as positive among the population, perceived as reasonable to increase a woman's health through a long tradition, conducted collectively throughout entire communities of the different surrounding countries, and obtained through severe pain on the part of the infant. Female circumcision is seen as a sacred concession that is the correct course of action to living a positive life.[298] The majority of people in sub-Saharan Africa find their own "causes" for why the tradition still

---

36. [296] Cialdini, Robert B. Chapter 3: Commitment and Consistency (52-95). *Influence: Science and practice.* 4th ed., 21st Century Bks, 2002.

37. [297] Cialdini, Robert B. Chapter 3: Commitment and Consistency (52-95). *Influence: Science and practice.* 4th ed., 21st Century Bks, 2002.

38. [298] Cialdini, Robert B. Chapter 2: Reciprocation (19-50). *Influence: Science and practice.* 4th ed., 21st Century Bks, 2002.

exists despite being illegal in some of these countries.[299] Through their own judgmental heuristics and cultural biases, they create "causes" that seem reasonable within their worldview and many people within sub-Saharan Africa have simply never thought deeply about female circumcision not being practiced in other parts of the world.[300][301] Sadly, many of these "causes" may be defended by scientists in their region who disingenuously represent the facts to defend the tribalism that they have a bias for within their home countries; thus, creating confusion and doubt from what would ordinarily be expert opinion because of cultural and theological induced blindness.

39. [299] Kahneman, Daniel. Chapter 6:"Norms, Surprises, and Causes" (71-78). *Thinking, fast and slow*. Farrar, Straus and Giroux, 2015.

40. [300] Kahneman, Daniel. Chapter 8: How Judgments Happen (89-96). *Thinking, fast and slow*. Farrar, Straus and Giroux, 2015.

41. [301] Kahneman, Daniel. Chapter 6:"Norms, Surprises, and Causes" (71-78). *Thinking, fast and slow*. Farrar, Straus and Giroux, 2015.

In a 1990 New York Times article, Melvin Konner lays out the consequences of this religious belief for young girls based on Klein's research from an interview with Klein:

> Between 90 million and 100 million women of all ages now living in Africa had their childhoods interrupted by a traditional operation in which the clitoris is partly or, more commonly, completely removed - without anesthesia, with crude cutting tools and with little or no precaution against infection. In most cases clitoral excision is followed by another operation, in which the labia are partly cut away and then sewn together. Once a girl has healed, her vagina is almost completely sealed, leaving her a "pinhole" opening, only large enough for urine to pass drop by drop.

> The immediate consequences of this operation sometimes include hemorrhage, tetanus and other infections, excruciating pain and death. More common results include painful urination, backup of menstrual blood and severe pain during sexual intercourse. (Two to 12 weeks are required for gradual penetration, which is essentially a process of repeated tearing; for convenience, the honeymoon hotel in the Sudanese city of Port Sudan is next to a hospital.) Traditionally women are resewn after the birth of each child ("renewable virginity") only to experience the same effects again.[302]

42. [302] Konner, Melvin. "MUTILATED IN THE NAME OF TRADITION." *The New York Times*, The New York Times, 14 Apr. 1990, www.nytimes.com/1990/04/15/books/mutilated-in-the-name-of-tradition.html.

Male Genital Mutilation

I apologize if this topic gives you any degree of discomfort and none of the following is an attempt to shame people who have undergone this procedure. I ask that – whatever your personal feelings and opinions on the matter – that you please read this section to its totality before forming a judgment about this issue and try to maintain impartiality to the best of your ability.

Circumcision is a physical representation of the commitment to self-contempt for the sake of a higher purpose.[303] It attempts to posit a rational basis that has been overwhelmingly discredited by recent scientific studies. Male circumcision has been disingenuously represented as a credible and rational medical procedure for male babies to undergo. After researching the topic, I've found that apologists of circumcision have promoted the most miniscule benefits and have gone so far as to use methodologically flawed studies to

---

43. [303] Nietzsche, Friedrich Wilhelm. *On the genealogy of morals: a polemical tract.* Translated by Ian Johnston, PDF, Richer Resources Publications, 2014.

promote circumcision throughout sub-Saharan Africa, Israel, and the

United States. Europe abandoned the practice long ago and has

conducted scientific studies that have given a less favorable portrayal

of circumcision than what the United States espouses. Believers of

circumcision try to utilize negligible and false scientific reasoning to

defend male genital mutilation; the CDC uses circumcision on the

basis of methodologically flawed tests that were never completed.[304]

They purported to run three studies in Africa to see if male

circumcision could prevent sexually transmitted infections, then

cancelled the study before the full data was collected during the time

circumcised men had to wait a week after the circumcisions before

they could report if they had contracted a sexually transmitted

infection, and then the CDC used the cancelled research study to

argue that circumcision prevented sexually transmitted infections.[305]

---

44. [304] Narvaez, Darcia. "More Circumcision Myths You May Believe: Hygiene and STDs." *Psychology Today*, Sussex Publishers, 13 Sept. 2011, www.psychologytoday.com/blog/moral-landscapes/201109/more-circumcision-myths-you-may-believe-hygiene-and-stds.

45. [305] Narvaez, Darcia. "More Circumcision Myths You May Believe: Hygiene and STDs." *Psychology Today*, Sussex Publishers, 13 Sept. 2011, www.psychologytoday.com/blog/moral-landscapes/201109/more-circumcision-myths-you-may-believe-hygiene-and-stds.

Findings by the CDC showing "consistency" since then have relied on the methodologically flawed testing as a basis. Doctors and nurses can legally lie to parents about the horrific trauma that their babies go through to continue gaining money from the surgical procedure.[306] People in the US and Canada have substituted religion with culture as the reasoning behind allowing their children to suffer physical and mental torment. Trauma has been shown by scientific studies that compared circumcised and uncircumcised babies. The belief that the nervous system isn't fully developed in babies upon birth is found to be a major myth among physicians from the research by more modern studies, babies suffer greater pain due to no anesthesia, and babies who don't cry during the procedure may be suffering intense shock.[307][308] Intense crying fits can be dangerous for the health of

46. [306] Narvaez, Darcia. "Circumcision's Psychological Damage." *Psychology Today*, Sussex Publishers, 11 Jan. 2015, www.psychologytoday.com/blog/moral-landscapes/201501/circumcision-s-psychological-damage.

47. [307] Goldman, R. "The psychological impact of circumcision." *Circumcision Resource Center*, THE CIRCUMCISION REFERENCE LIBRARY, www.cirp.org/library/psych/goldman1/.

48. [308] Page, Gayle Giboney. "Are There Long-Term Consequences of Pain in

infants, one infant ruptured their stomach from excessive crying and

Canadian doctors conducting studies on the matter of circumcision

state there is no question that babies who undergo circumcision suffer

intense pain.[309] They're likely to suffer future trauma at a certain

point in their lives that happen anywhere from early child care to old

age; a recent controversial study has linked circumcision with

autism.[310][311] Furthermore, circumcision can cause intense bleeding,

the spread of infections on the penis, and surgical accidents can result

in medical professionals being forced to amputate the penis

entirely.[312] Deaths of infants as a result of the circumcision procedure

Newborn or Very Young Infants?" *The Journal of Perinatal Education*, U.S. National Library of Medicine, 2004, www.ncbi.nlm.nih.gov/pmc/articles/PMC1595204/.

49. [309] "Infant Responses to Circumcision." *Circumcision Resource Center*, circumcision.org/infant-responses-to-circumcision/.

50. [310] Freeman, David. "Circumcision Linked To Autism In Controversial New Study." *The Huffington Post*, TheHuffingtonPost.com, 20 Jan. 2015, www.huffingtonpost.com/2015/01/20/circumcision-autism-new-study_n_6503106.html.

51. [311] Kovac, Sarah. "New autism dispute: is circumcision a factor?" *Time*, Time, time.com/4314388/new-autism-dispute-is-circumcision-a-factor/.

52. [312] Boyle, G. J. "Issues associated with the introduction of circumcision into a non-Circumcising society." *Issues associated with the introduction of circumcision into a non-Circumcising society*, THE CIRCUMCISION

have also occurred.[313] The supposed benefits against HIV are based on dubious studies that didn't even attempt to research circumcision on infants.[314] Attempts at defending circumcision only show the primitive nature of North American and Middle Eastern culture. Circumcision is male genital mutilation and the practice itself is no different than Africa's female genital mutilation of young girls.[315] Arguably, the US and Canada conducting such behavior despite higher educational institutions and a higher quality of life shows how egregious this contemptuous practice truly is. It is worse because Canadians and Americans have the ability of knowing better.

REFERENCE LIBRARY, Nov. 2003,
www.cirp.org/library/disease/HIV/boyle-sti/.

53. [313] Boyle, G. J. "Issues associated with the introduction of circumcision into a non-Circumcising society." *Issues associated with the introduction of circumcision into a non-Circumcising society*, THE CIRCUMCISION REFERENCE LIBRARY, Nov. 2003, www.cirp.org/library/disease/HIV/boyle-sti/.

54. [314] Myers, A, and J Myers. *Rolling out male circumcision as a mass HIV/AIDS intervention seems neither justified nor practicable*, www.cirp.org/library/disease/HIV/myers2008/.

55. [315] "About Us." *Doctors Opposing Circumcision*, www.doctorsopposingcircumcision.org/about-us/#_statement-principles.

The South African Medical Journal in a 2008 article lists several methodology and ethical issues with the circumcision studies conducted by the US that raise concerns on the dubious nature of US studies that claim male circumcision reduces sexually transmitted infections. The acronym MC refers to male circumcision for the purposes of the journal:

The 2003 Cochrane review[5] of observational studies of MC effectiveness concluded that there was insufficient evidence to support it as an anti-HIV intervention. Three randomised controlled trials (RCTs) from South Africa, Kenya and Uganda in 2006 - 2007 show a protective effect of MC. However, Garenne[6] has subsequently shown from observational data that there is considerable heterogeneity of the effect of MC across 14 African countries. Despite the South African RCT showing a protective effect, he reports for the nine South African provinces that 'there is no evidence that HIV transmission over the period 1994 - 2004 was slower in those provinces with higher levels of circumcision'. Interestingly, in both Kenya and Uganda, where two of the RCTs were done, a protective effect of MC was observed, but a harmful effect was observed in Cameroon, Lesotho and Malawi. The other eight countries showed no significant effect of MC.

These somewhat discordant findings are difficult to interpret. While RCTs are theoretically strong designs, it is conceivable that their findings are not generalisable beyond their settings. Furthermore, there have been no trials of neonatal MC. Study flaws such as inability to obtain double blinding, and loss to follow-up in RCTs, may effectively degrade their quality to that of observational studies. Meanwhile other disturbing findings referred to by Sidler *et al.* are emerging, including the reported higher risk for women partners of circumcised HIV positive men, disinhibition, urological complications, relatively small effect sizes of MC at the population level, and relative cost-inefficiency of MC.

Not all objections to MC as an HIV intervention have to do with evidence of effectiveness or cost. Sidler *et al.* raise ethical objections. Owing to the current climate of desperation with regard to the HIV epidemic, evidence in favour of MC frequently seems overstated. This reduces the scope for informed consent and autonomy for adult men considering the procedure. Further problems arise in the case of neonates whose parents may be considering the procedure. Whereas informed consent is at least possible for adult men, it is clearly not possible for neonates. Parents can only guess what the child's wishes would be if he were presented with the information they have at their disposal. If it could be shown that circumcision was necessary in the neonatal period, parental consent on behalf of the neonate would be justified. But since no valid surgical indications for circumcision exist in this period, and the future benefit to the child in respect of HIV avoidance is not relevant before sexual debut, the duty of parents may well be to err on the side of caution, and defer the procedure until the child can make an autonomous decision. In the absence of compelling indications, a procedure such as circumcision could also be seen as a violation of the child's right to bodily integrity. Furthermore, the ethical principle of non-maleficence cannot be upheld as there are clear harms attached to this practice, to which Sidler *et al.* refer in their article. Lastly, at a societal level MC may be unjust insofar as it could compete for resources with more effective and less costly interventions[7] and disadvantage women.[316]

Several studies conducted in Denmark show alarming problems with circumcision that the United States has seen fit to uniformly ignore but which the US public, the public of the various African countries, and religious groups that practice circumcision should take into serious consideration before conducting such a surgery on their infant children.

---

56. [316] Myers, J. "Male circumcision and HIV infection." *History of Circumcision*, Historyofcircumcision.net, www.historyofcircumcision.net/index.php?option=content&task=view&id =85.

In one cross-sectional study that was titled "*Male*

Circumcision and sexual function in men and women", the study

found that circumcised men had frequent orgasm difficulties and their

female spouses were less sexually satisfied:

RESULTS:
Age at first intercourse, perceived importance of a good sex life and
current sexual activity differed little between circumcised and
uncircumcised men or between women with circumcised and
uncircumcised spouses. However, circumcised men reported more partners
and were more likely to report frequent orgasm difficulties after adjustment
for potential confounding factors [11 vs 4%, OR(adj) = 3.26; 95%
confidence interval (CI) 1.42-7.47], and women with circumcised spouses
more often reported incomplete sexual needs fulfilment (38 vs 28%,
OR(adj) = 2.09; 95% CI 1.05-4.16) and frequent sexual function
difficulties overall (31 vs 22%, OR(adj) = 3.26; 95% CI 1.15-9.27), notably
orgasm difficulties (19 vs 14%, OR(adj) = 2.66; 95% CI 1.07-6.66) and
dyspareunia (12 vs 3%, OR(adj) = 8.45; 95% CI 3.01-23.74). Findings
were stable in several robustness analyses, including one restricted to non-
Jews and non-Moslems.

CONCLUSIONS:
Circumcision was associated with frequent orgasm difficulties in Danish
men and with a range of frequent sexual difficulties in women, notably
orgasm difficulties, dyspareunia and a sense of incomplete sexual needs
fulfilment. Thorough examination of these matters in areas where male
circumcision is more common is warranted.[317]

In a Danish 2015 study, titled: "*Ritual Circumcision and risk*

of autism spectrum disorder in 0 to 9 year-old boys", Danish

---

57. [317] Frisch, M, et al. "Male circumcision and sexual function in men and
women: a survey-Based, cross-Sectional study in Denmark." *International
journal of epidemiology.*, U.S. National Library of Medicine, Oct. 2011,
www.ncbi.nlm.nih.gov/pubmed/21672947.

researchers have confirmed a causal link between circumcision and the increase in autism in young boys. Circumcised boys were statistically higher in being diagnosed with autism spectrum disorder (ASD). The findings were as follows:

Abstract

Objective

Based on converging observations in animal, clinical and ecological studies, we hypothesised a possible impact of ritual circumcision on the subsequent risk of autism spectrum disorder (ASD) in young boys.

Design

National, register-based cohort study.

Setting

Denmark.

Participants

A total of 342,877 boys born between 1994 and 2003 and followed in the age span 0–9 years between 1994 and 2013.

Main outcome measures

Information about cohort members' ritual circumcisions, confounders and ASD outcomes, as well as two supplementary

251

outcomes, hyperkinetic disorder and asthma, was obtained from national registers. Hazard ratios (HRs) with 95% confidence intervals (CIs) associated with foreskin status were obtained using Cox proportional hazards regression analyses.

Results

With a total of 4986 ASD cases, our study showed that regardless of cultural background circumcised boys were more likely than intact boys to develop ASD before age 10 years (HR = 1.46; 95% CI: 1.11–1.93). Risk was particularly high for infantile autism before age five years (HR = 2.06; 95% CI: 1.36–3.13). Circumcised boys in non-Muslim families were also more likely to develop hyperkinetic disorder (HR = 1.81; 95% CI: 1.11–2.96). Associations with asthma were consistently inconspicuous (HR = 0.96; 95% CI: 0.84–1.10).

Conclusions

We confirmed our hypothesis that boys who undergo ritual circumcision may run a greater risk of developing ASD. This finding, and the unexpected observation of an increased risk of hyperactivity disorder among circumcised boys in non-Muslim families, need attention, particularly because data limitations most likely rendered our HR estimates conservative. Considering the widespread practice of non-therapeutic circumcision in infancy and childhood around the world, confirmatory studies should be given priority.[318]

---

58. [318] Frisch, Morten, and Jacob Simonsen. "Ritual circumcision and risk of autism spectrum disorder in 0- to 9-Year-Old boys: national cohort study in Denmark." *Journal of the Royal Society of Medicine*, vol. 108, no. 7, Aug. 2015, pp. 266–279., doi:10.1177/0141076814565942.

The true reason for male circumcision, for the most part, is the belief that circumcision will grant entrance to the Kingdom of God in the Abrahamic faiths. A principal belief that Jews, Muslims, and certain Christian denominations believe are necessary for their faith. This primitive tribalism conducted during our modern age shows the pernicious effects of religious thinking because of how normalized the damaging of the genitals is for Abrahamic culture. Circumcision is found to decrease penile sensitivity and decrease the pleasure of orgasm for men.[319] It is truly disturbing to acknowledge and the disingenuous pseudo-scientific arguments supporting this for the sake of a higher power shows the true cruelty that religion invokes from parent to child. The original study arguing about the so-called benefits of circumcision was cancelled before it was completed and there has never been a reproduction of the results; it isn't surprising since the scientific experiment was never completed. To reiterate: the US government conducted the experiment on three different African villages and the CDC has argued its supposed benefits but non-

---

59. [319] Bronselaer, G A, et al. "Male circumcision decreases penile sensitivity as measured in a large cohort." *BJU international.*, U.S. National Library of Medicine, May 2013, www.ncbi.nlm.nih.gov/pubmed/23374102.

government health organizations have found the claims dubious

because of how flawed the methodology was.[320] Circumcised men

had to wait weeks after their operation to conduct normal sexual

behavior and the "results" were obtained before any completion of the

study. The data was used as a basis to defend circumcision despite

these grave issues regarding the legitimacy of the experiment. In

particular, the lack of repeated experiments and the overemphasis on

the mutilation practice lowering urinary tract infection – which is

lowered to about 1 percent, is negligible. By comparison, breast

cancer for women has a rate of 12 percent but we don't remove

women's breasts to protect them from a miniscule percentage of

risk.[321] Male circumcision, despite existing prior to the Abrahamic

traditions, is an intrinsic part of Judaism, Islam, and denominations of

Christianity. Jews, certain Christians, and Muslims believe that

circumcision is necessary to enter the Kingdom of God and the

---

60. [321] Narvaez, Darcia. "More Circumcision Myths You May Believe: Hygiene and STDs." *Psychology Today*, Sussex Publishers, 13 Sept. 2011, www.psychologytoday.com/blog/moral-landscapes/201109/more-circumcision-myths-you-may-believe-hygiene-and-stds.

practice is conducted because of this theological basis. Doctors

throughout the United States, Africa, and the Middle East may have

substituted the initial reasons for circumcision - to make masturbation

less pleasurable for men - to arguing "health benefits" to stay

consistent with their religious practices and cultural norms via

substituting the original reasons with confirmation bias towards any

positive benefits.[322] From all of the research that I've looked into and

the findings of medical professionals, the foreskin is a completely

healthy part of the male anatomy that doesn't need to be removed.[323]

Shaming men for having foreskin or shaming parents for not having

their child's foreskin removed seems to be a cultural tradition of

misandry that comes from antiquated cultural norms of the Abrahamic

faiths.[324]

---

61. [322] Kahneman, Daniel. Chapter 9: Answering an Easier Question (97-104). *Thinking, fast and slow*. Farrar, Straus and Giroux, 2015.

62. [323] "About Us." *Doctors Opposing Circumcision*, www.doctorsopposingcircumcision.org/about-us/#_statement-principles.

63. [324] Green, Laci. "I LOVE FORESKIN (Wtf circumcision?)." *YouTube*, YouTube, 14 Aug. 2013, www.youtube.com/watch?v=JbTdkWV89Ak.

Bibliography

Preface

1. "Atheism Doubles Among Generation Z." *Barna Group*, www.barna.com/research/atheism-doubles-among-generation-z/.
2. Baggini, Julian. "Atheists, Please Read My Heathen Manifesto | Julian Baggini." *The Guardian*, Guardian News and Media, 25 Mar. 2012, www.theguardian.com/commentisfree/2012/mar/25/atheists-please-read-heathen-manifesto.
3. Birkenhead, Peter. "Why Do We Let New Atheists and Religious Zealots Dominate the Conversation about Religion?" *Salon*, Salon.com, 27 Apr. 2015, www.salon.com/2015/04/25/why_do_we_let_new_atheists_and_religious_zealots_dominate_the_conversation_about_religion/.
4. Bruenig, Elizabeth. "Is the New Atheism Dead?" *The New Republic*, 4 Nov. 2015, newrepublic.com/article/123349/new-atheism-dead.
5. Cep, Casey. "Why Are Americans Still Uncomfortable with Atheism?" *The New Yorker*, The New Yorker, 24 Apr. 2019, www.newyorker.com/magazine/2018/10/29/why-are-americans-still-uncomfortable-with-atheism.
6. Cox, Daniel. "Way More Americans May Be Atheists Than We Thought." *FiveThirtyEight*, FiveThirtyEight, 18 May 2017, fivethirtyeight.com/features/way-more-americans-may-be-atheists-than-we-thought/.
7. Dryden, Windy. *Overcoming Procrastination*. Sheldon, 2000.
8. England, Charlotte. "The Reason Why Atheists Are More Intelligent than Religious People, According to Researchers." *The Independent*, Independent Digital News and Media, 2 Jan. 2018, www.independent.co.uk/news/science/atheists-more-intelligent-than-religious-people-faith-instinct-cleverness-a7742766.html.
9. Gauthier, Brendan. "Never Tweet, Richard Dawkins: Famed Atheist Now Signal-Boosting Nazi Propaganda." *Salon*, Salon.com, 1 Feb. 2016, www.salon.com/2016/02/01/never_tweet_richard_dawkins_famed_atheist_now_signal_boosting_nazi_propaganda/.
10. Gray, John. "What Scares the New Atheists | John Gray." *The Guardian*, Guardian News and Media, 3 Mar. 2015, www.theguardian.com/world/2015/mar/03/what-scares-the-new-atheists.
11. Green, Emma. "The Origins of Aggressive Atheism." *The Atlantic*, Atlantic Media Company, 24 Nov. 2014, www.theatlantic.com/national/archive/2014/11/the-origins-of-aggressive-atheism/383088/.
12. Greenwald, Glenn. "Sam Harris, the New Atheists, and Anti-Muslim

Animus | Glenn Greenwald." *The Guardian*, Guardian News and Media, 3 Apr. 2013, www.theguardian.com/commentisfree/2013/apr/03/sam-harris-muslim-animus.

13. Halla, Barbara. "New Atheism: Missing the Point." *Harvard Political Review New Atheism Missing the Point* , 7 May 2012, harvardpolitics.com/books-arts/new-atheism-missing-the-point/.

14. Hamburger, Jacob. "What Was New Atheism?" *The Point Magazine*, 25 Jan. 2019, thepointmag.com/2019/politics/what-was-new-atheism.

15. Hedges, Chris. "Fundamentalism Kills." *Truthdig*, 26 July 2011, www.truthdig.com/articles/fundamentalism-kills/.

16. Hitchens, Christopher. "Christopher Hitchens Get Waterboarded | Vanity Fair." *YouTube*, Vanity Fair, 2 July 2008, www.youtube.com/watch?v=4LPubUCJv58.

17. Hitchens, Christopher. "Christopher Hitchens: Hell's Angel: Mother Teresa (English Subtitles)." *YouTube*, BBC News, 7 Jan. 2015, youtu.be/NK7l_IhtKNU.

18. Hitchens, Christopher. "The Dark Side Of Religion | Christopher Hitchens @ FreedomFest." *YouTube*, FFreeThinker, 25 Apr. 2009, www.youtube.com/watch?v=iooXQ1-P-0s.

19. Hobson, Theo. "Richard Dawkins Has Lost: Meet the New New Atheists." *The Spectator*, 12 Apr. 2013, www.spectator.co.uk/2013/04/after-the-new-atheism/.

20. Hoelscher, David. "New Atheism, Worse Than You Think." *CounterPunch.org*, 1 Feb. 2016, www.counterpunch.org/2016/01/29/new-atheism-worse-than-you-think/.

21. "How World Hijab Day Harms Women." *YouTube*, Genetically Modified Skeptic, 1 Feb. 2019, www.youtube.com/watch?v=vVpZ0FZc8SY.

22. Hussain, Murtaza. "Scientific Racism, Militarism, and the New Atheists." *Israel | Al Jazeera*, Al Jazeera, 2 Apr. 2013, www.aljazeera.com/indepth/opinion/2013/04/20134210413618256.html.

23. Lean, Nathan. "Dawkins, Harris, Hitchens: New Atheists Flirt with Islamophobia." *Salon*, Salon.com, 29 Mar. 2013, www.salon.com/2013/03/30/dawkins_harris_hitchens_new_atheists_flirt_with_islamophobia/.

24. Megoran, Nick, and Russell Foster. "Why the Arguments of the 'New Atheists' Are Often Just as Violent as Religion." *The Conversation*, 19 Sept. 2018, theconversation.com/why-the-arguments-of-the-new-atheists-are-often-just-as-violent-as-religion-95185.

25. Mitchell, Travis. "Young Adults around the World Are Less Religious." *Pew Research Center's Religion & Public Life Project*, Pew Research Center's Religion & Public Life Project, 13 June 2018, www.pewforum.org/2018/06/13/young-adults-around-the-world-are-less-religious-by-several-measures/.

26. Murphy, Ian. "Five Atheists Who Ruin It for Everyone Else." *Salon*, Salon.com, 5 Aug. 2012, www.salon.com/2012/08/04/five_most_awful_atheists_salpart/.
27. Niose, David. "Misinformation and Facts about Secularism and Religion." *Psychology Today*, Sussex Publishers, www.psychologytoday.com/us/blog/our-humanity-naturally/201103/misinformation-and-facts-about-secularism-and-religion.
28. "Non-Believers Do Not Lack Morality, Research Suggests." *ITV News*, www.itv.com/news/2019-05-27/non-believers-do-not-lack-morality-research-suggests/?fbclid=IwAR0CmMEZONwS4OqRFotigWhhLP9i1MUbkGOUvp0RoWVGb4acADr2QGSDlDg
29. Poole, Steven. "The Four Horsemen Review - Whatever Happened to 'New Atheism'?" *The Guardian*, Guardian News and Media, 31 Jan. 2019, www.theguardian.com/books/2019/jan/31/four-horsemen-review-what-happened-to-new-atheism-dawkins-hitchens.
30. Robertson, Eleanor. "Richard Dawkins, What on Earth Happened to You? | Eleanor Robertson." *The Guardian*, Guardian News and Media, 30 July 2014, www.theguardian.com/commentisfree/2014/jul/30/richard-dawkins-what-on-earth-happened-to-you.
31. Sherwood, Harriet. "Religious Children Are Meaner than Their Secular Counterparts, Study Finds." *The Guardian*, Guardian News and Media, 6 Nov. 2015, www.theguardian.com/world/2015/nov/06/religious-children-less-altruistic-secular-kids-study.
32. Sparrow, Jeff. "We Can Save Atheism from the New Atheists like Richard Dawkins | Jeff Sparrow." *The Guardian*, Guardian News and Media, 29 Nov. 2015, www.theguardian.com/commentisfree/2015/nov/30/we-can-save-atheism-from-the-new-atheists.
33. Torres, Phil. "How Did 'New Atheism' Slide so Far toward the Alt-Right?" *Salon*, Salon.com, 29 July 2017, www.salon.com/2017/07/29/from-the-enlightenment-to-the-dark-ages-how-new-atheism-slid-into-the-alt-right/.
34. West, Ed. "New Atheism Is Dead." *Catholic Herald*, 4 Mar. 2013, catholicherald.co.uk/commentandblogs/2013/03/04/whatever-happened-to-new-atheism/.
35. Xygalatas, Dimitris. "Are Religious People More Moral?" *Religion News Service*, 25 Oct. 2017, religionnews.com/2017/10/25/are-religious-people-more-moral/.

Chapter 1

1. Barker, Jeff. "Statisticians question logic of buying multiple lottery tickets

as jackpot rises to $1.5 B." *Baltimoresun.com*, 13 Jan. 2016,
www.baltimoresun.com/business/bs-bz-powerball-maryland-odds-
20160111-story.html.

2. Boseley, Sarah. "How Bill and Melinda Gates helped save 122m lives –
    and what they want to solve next." *The Guardian*, Guardian News and
    Media, 14 Feb. 2017, www.theguardian.com/world/2017/feb/14/bill-gates-
    philanthropy-warren-buffett-vaccines-infant-mortality.

3. "CASTLE ROCK V. GONZALES." *Legal Information Institute*, Cornell
    University Law School, 21 Mar. 2005,
    www.law.cornell.edu/supct/html/04-278.ZS.html.

4. CHEDEKEL, LISA , et al. "Haditha: Marine Linked To Civilian Deaths
    Was A Quiet Honor Student, Friends Say." *Hartford Courant*, 3 June
    2006, articles.courant.com/2006-06-03/news/0606030586_1_frank-
    wuterich-haditha-squad-leader. I had initially hoped to use a Huffington
    Post article that described Frank Wuterich as a family man in conjunction
    with this, but it seems to have been removed.

5. Cialdini, Robert B. *Influence: Science and practice.* 4th ed., 21st Century
    Bks, 2002. Chapter 1: Weapons of Influence (1-16), Chapter 3:
    Commitment and Consistency (52-95), Chapter 4: Social Proof (98-140),
    Chapter 6: Authority (178-200)

6. "Facts Statistics: Mortality risk." *Facts Statistics: Mortality risk | III*,
    www.iii.org/fact-statistic/facts-statistics-mortality-risk.

7. "Full text: bin Laden's 'letter to America'." *The Guardian*, Guardian News
    and Media, 24 Nov. 2002,
    www.theguardian.com/world/2002/nov/24/theobserver.

8. Gause, F. Gregory . "Getting It Backward on Iraq." *Foreign Affairs*,
    Foreign Affairs, 28 Jan. 2009, www.foreignaffairs.com/articles/iraq/1999-
    05-01/getting-it-backward-iraq.

9. Goldberg, Philip. "Missionaries in India: Conversion or Coercion?" *The
    Huffington Post*, TheHuffingtonPost.com, 19 Feb. 2014,
    www.huffingtonpost.com/philip-goldberg/missionaries-in-
    india_b_4470448.html

10. Greenhouse, Linda. "Justices Rule Police Do Not Have a Constitutional
    Duty to Protect Someone." *The New York Times*, The New York Times, 28
    June 2005, www.nytimes.com/2005/06/28/politics/justices-rule-police-do-
    not-have-a-constitutional-duty-to-protect.html.

11. Hackett, Conrad, and David McClendon. "World's Largest Religion by
    Population Is Still Christianity." *Pew Research Center*, Pew Research
    Center, 5 Apr. 2017, www.pewresearch.org/fact-
    tank/2017/04/05/christians-remain-worlds-largest-religious-group-but-
    they-are-declining-in-europe/.

12. Hedges, Chris. *War Is a Force That Gives Us Meaning*. PublicAffairs,
    2002.

13. Isidore, Chris. "These are your odds of winning Powerball or Mega Millions." *CNNMoney*, Cable News Network, money.cnn.com/2018/01/04/news/powerball-mega-millions-odds/index.html.

14. Ispas, Alexa. *Psychology and politics: a social identity perspective*. Psychology Press, 2014. For reference purposes: Chapter 1: Psychology and the Social Identity Perspective (1-24), Chapter 2: The Psychology of Social Influence (26-50).

15. Kahneman, Daniel. *Thinking, fast and slow*. Farrar, Straus and Giroux, 2015. For reference purposes: The Introduction (1-17), Chapter 4: The Associative Machine (50-58), Chapter 5: Cognitive Ease (59-70), Chapter 6:"Norms, Surprises, and Causes" (71-78), Chapter 7: A Machine for Jumping to Conclusions (79-88), Chapter 8: How Judgments Happen (89-96), Chapter 9: Answering an Easier Question (97-107), Chapter 11: Anchors (119-128), Chapter 12: The Science of Availability (129-136), Chapter 13: Availability, Emotion, and Risk (137-145), Chapter 19: The Illusion of Understanding (199-208), Chapter 20: The Illusion of Validity (209-221), and Chapter 28: Bad Events (300-309).

16. McDermott, Rose. *Political Psychology in International Relations*. Ann Arbor: U of Michigan, 2004. Print. For reference: Chapter 4: Cognition and Attitudes (77-117), Chapter 5: Do Actions Speak Louder Than Words? (119-152).

17. Merritt, Jonathan. "Insisting Jesus Was White Is Bad History and Bad Theology." *The Atlantic*, Atlantic Media Company, 12 Dec. 2013, www.theatlantic.com/politics/archive/2013/12/insisting-jesus-was-white-is-bad-history-and-bad-theology/282310/.

18. Morgan, Piers. *YouTube*, CNN, 7 Jan. 2013, www.youtube.com/watch?v=ror9v2LwHoY.

19. Nietzsche, Friedrich Wilhelm. *THE ANTICHRIST*. Translated by H. L. Mencken, The Project Gutenberg, 2006. For reference: Aphorism 40 and 41.

20. No. 04-278 TOWN OF CASTLE ROCK, COLORADO v. JESSICA GONZALES. https://www.justice.gov/sites/default/files/osg/briefs/2004/01/01/2004-0278.mer.ami.pdf 1-45. Supreme Court of the United States. 27 June 2005.*Justice.Gov*. United States, 27 June 2005. Web. 5 Feb. 2018. <https://www.justice.gov/sites/default/files/osg/briefs/2004/01/01/2004-0278.mer.ami.pdf>.

21. O'Brien, Matt. "Why you should never, ever play the lottery." *The Washington Post*, WP Company, 14 May 2015, www.washingtonpost.com/news/wonk/wp/2015/05/14/why-you-should-never-ever-play-the-lottery/?utm_term=.60541de1ad73.

22. Pelley, Scott. "Haditha massacre defendant: We did what we had to." *CBS*

News, CBS Interactive, 6 Jan. 2012, www.cbsnews.com/news/haditha-massacre-defendant-we-did-what-we-had-to/.

23. Puente, Mark. "Sun Investigates: Undue force." *The Baltimore Sun*, 28 Sept. 2014, data.baltimoresun.com/news/police-settlements/.

24. Roser, Max. "Visual History of The Rise of Political Freedom and the Decrease in Violence." *Visual History of The Rise of Political Freedom and the Decrease in Violence*. Web. 3 Jan. 2016.

25. Rubenstein, J. "Cannibals and Crusaders." *French Historical Studies*, vol. 31, no. 4, Jan. 2008, pp. 525–552., doi:10.1215/00161071-2008-005. PDF.

26. Teitelbaum, Joel, et al. "Town Of Castle Rock, Colorado V. Gonzales: Implications for Public Health Policy and Practice." *Public Health Reports*, Association of Schools of Public Health, 2006, www.ncbi.nlm.nih.gov/pmc/articles/PMC1525280/.

27. "The Changing Global Religious Landscape." *Pew Research Center's Religion & Public Life Project*, Pew Research Center's Religion & Public Life Project, 26 July 2017, www.pewforum.org/2017/04/05/the-changing-global-religious-landscape/.

28. Walton, D. N. "Appeal to Popularity." *Https://Www.logicallyfallacious.com*, www.logicallyfallacious.com/tools/lp/Bo/LogicalFallacies/40/Appeal-to-Popularity.

Chapter 2

1. Boseley, Sarah. "How Bill and Melinda Gates helped save 122m lives – and what they want to solve next." *The Guardian*, Guardian News and Media, 14 Feb. 2017, www.theguardian.com/world/2017/feb/14/bill-gates-philanthropy-warren-buffett-vaccines-infant-mortality.

2. Camp, Jim. "Decisions Are Emotional, Not Logical: the Neuroscience behind Decision Making." *Big Think*, Big Think, 11 June 2012, bigthink.com/experts-corner/decisions-are-emotional-not-logical-the-neuroscience-behind-decision-making.

3. Cialdini, Robert B. *Influence: Science and practice.* 4th ed., 21st Century Bks, 2002. For reference: Chapter 4: Social Proof (98-140).

4. Cooper, Spring Chenoa, and Anthony J. Santellla. "Happy news! Masturbation actually has health benefits." *The Conversation*, 5 Dec. 2017, theconversation.com/happy-news-masturbation-actually-has-health-benefits-16539.

5. Freeman, Daniel, and Jason Freeman. "Why are men more likely than women to take their own lives?" *The Guardian*, Guardian News and Media, 21 Jan. 2015, www.theguardian.com/science/2015/jan/21/suicide-gender-men-women-mental-health-nick-clegg.

6. Galef, Julia. "The Straw Vulcan, Julia Galef Skepticon 4." *YouTube*, YouTube, 17 Aug. 2013, www.youtube.com/watch?v=Fv1nMc-k0N4.

7. Gates, Bill. *YouTube*, Thegatesnotes, 5 Jan. 2015, www.youtube.com/watch?v=bVzppWSIFU0.

8. Gates, Bill, and Melinda Gates. "Warren Buffett's Best Investment." *Gatesnotes.com*, Bill and Melinda Gates, 14 Feb. 2017, www.gatesnotes.com/2017-Annual-Letter.

9. Gittleson, Wendy. "Christian 'Soul Vultures' Are Exploiting The Nepal Earthquake 'For Christ' (VIDEO)." *AddictingInfo*, 27 Apr. 2015, addictinginfo.com/2015/04/27/christian-soul-vultures-are-exploiting-the-nepal-earthquake-for-christ-video/.

10. Hedges, Chris. *War Is a Force That Gives Us Meaning*. PublicAffairs, 2002.

11. Hitchens, Christopher. "Christopher Hitchens: Hell's Angel: Mother Teresa (English Subtitles)." *YouTube*, BBC News, 7 Jan. 2015, youtu.be/NK7l_IhtKNU.

12. Ispas, Alexa. *Psychology and politics: a social identity perspective*. Psychology Press, 2014.

13. Jentleson, Bruce W. *American foreign policy: the dynamics of choice in the 21st century*. 4th ed., Norton, 2010. Chapter 1: The Strategic Context: Foreign Policy Strategy and the Essence of Choice (2-26), Readings for Part 1 Power by Hans J. Morgenthau (198-201)

14. Kahneman, Daniel. *Thinking, fast and slow*. Farrar, Straus and Giroux, 2015. For reference purposes: Chapter 5: Cognitive Ease (59-70).

15. "Masturbation Side Effects and Benefits." *Healthline*, Healthline Media, www.healthline.com/health/masturbation-side-effects.

16. "Masturbation | Get the Facts About Masturbation Health." *Planned Parenthood*, Planned Parenthood, www.plannedparenthood.org/learn/sex-and-relationships/masturbation.

17. Neary, Sarah. "Forced to Convert: How American Missionaries Really Treat Indigenous Akha Children." *Intercontinental Cry*, IC, 23 Apr. 2013, intercontinentalcry.org/forced-to-convert-how-american-missionaries-really-treat-indigenous-akha-children/.

18. Neelakandan, Aravindan. "Why No Outrage over Conversion of Tsunami Victims?" *Swarajya*, 29 Dec. 2014, swarajyamag.com/politics/why-no-outrage-over-conversion-of-tsunami-victims.

19. Nietzsche, Friedrich Wilhelm. *Thus spake Zarathustra: a book for all and none*. Translated by Thomas Common, PDF ed., T. Common, 1908. Chapter IX: Preachers of Death (50-52), Chapter XXVI: THE PRIESTS (88-91)

20. Nietzsche, Friedrich Wilhelm. *THE ANTICHRIST*. Translated by H. L. Mencken, The Project Gutenberg, 2006. For reference: Aphorisms 15 and 16.

21. Nietzsche, Friedrich Wilhelm. *On the genealogy of morals: a polemical tract*. Translated by Ian Johnston, PDF, Richer Resources Publications, 2014.

22. Roser, Max. "Visual History of The Rise of Political Freedom and the Decrease in Violence." *Visual History of The Rise of Political Freedom and the Decrease in Violence*. Web. 3 Jan. 2016.

23. Viglianco-VanPelt, Michelle, and Kyla Boyse. "Masturbation." Edited by Jennifer Gold Christner, *University of Michigan Health System*, July 2009, www.med.umich.edu/yourchild/topics/masturb.htm.

24. Viotti, Paul R., and Mark V. Kauppi. *International relations theory: realism, pluralism, globalism*. 3rd ed., Macmillan, 1998.   For reference, Chapter 2: Realism: The State, Power, and the Balance of Power (55-197)

25. "When Nepal Was Groaning in Earthquake, Christian Missionaries Were Shamelessly Selling Jesus." *OpIndia*, 4 May 2015, www.opindia.com/2015/04/when-nepal-was-groaning-in-earthquake-christian-missionaries-were-shamelessly-selling-jesus/.

26. Yudkowsky, Eliezer. "What Do We Mean By "Rationality"?" *Less Wrong*, 16 Mar. 2009, lesswrong.com/lw/31/what_do_we_mean_by_rationality/.

Chapter 3

1. Carr, Kelly, and Scot J. Paltrow. "Reuters Investigates - UNACCOUNTABLE: The Pentagon's bad bookkeeping." *Reuters*, Thomson Reuters, 2 July 2013, www.reuters.com/investigates/pentagon/#article/part1.

2. Carr, Kelly, and Scot J. Paltrow. "Reuters Investigates - UNACCOUNTABLE: The Pentagon's bad bookkeeping." *Reuters*, Thomson Reuters, 2 July 2013, www.reuters.com/investigates/pentagon/#article/part2.

3. Carr, Kelly, and Scot J. Paltrow. "Reuters Investigates - UNACCOUNTABLE: The Pentagon's bad bookkeeping." *Reuters*, Thomson Reuters, 2 July 2013, www.reuters.com/investigates/pentagon/#article/part3.

4. "Circular Reasoning." *Https://Www.logicallyfallacious.com*, www.logicallyfallacious.com/tools/lp/Bo/LogicalFallacies/66/Circular-Reasoning.

5. Eggen, Dan, and Scott Wilson. "Suicide Bombs Potent Tools of Terrorists." *The Washington Post*, WP Company, 17 July 2005, www.washingtonpost.com/archive/politics/2005/07/17/suicide-bombs-potent-tools-of-terrorists/e11ed483-9936-45c0-b6c6-2653d4519ff5/?utm_term=.c23458392a4a.

6. Grinnell, Renée. "Just-World Hypothesis." *Encyclopedia of Psychology*, 17 July 2016, psychcentral.com/encyclopedia/just-world-hypothesis/.

7. Hitchens, Christopher. "Christopher Hitchens: Hell's Angel: Mother Teresa (English Subtitles)." *YouTube*, BBC News, 7 Jan. 2015, youtu.be/NK7l_IhtKNU.

8. Ispas, Alexa. *Psychology and politics: a social identity perspective*. Psychology Press, 2014.

9. Kahneman, Daniel. *Thinking, fast and slow*. Farrar, Straus and Giroux, 2015. For reference purposes: The Introduction (1-17), Chapter 6: Norms, Surprises, and Causes (71-78), Chapter 8: How Judgments Happen (89-96), Chapter 9: Answering an Easier Question (97-104), Chapter 29: The Fourfold Pattern (310-321), Chapter 30: Rare Events (322-333), Chapter 31: Risk Policies (334-341), and Chapter 32: Keeping Score (342 - 352)

10. Lankford, Adam. "Martyr myth: Inside the minds of suicide bombers." *New Scientist*, 3 July 2013, www.newscientist.com/article/mg21929240-200-martyr-myth-inside-the-minds-of-suicide-bombers/.

11. Lankford, Adam. "Exposing false 'martyrs' as suicidal." *The Jerusalem Post | JPost.Com*, 17 Feb. 2013, www.jpost.com/Opinion/Op-Ed-Contributors/Exposing-false-martyrs-as-suicidal.

12. Lankford, Adam. "What You Don't Understand about Suicide Attacks." *Scientific American*, 27 July 2015, www.scientificamerican.com/article/what-you-don-t-understand-about-suicide-attacks/.

13. Lester, David. "Female Suicide Bombers: Clues from Journalists." *Suicidology Online*, Suicidology Online, 14 Nov. 2011, www.suicidology-online.com/pdf/SOL-2011-2-62-66.pdf.

14. Lowe, Josh. "How Britain's history with the IRA made it resilient to attacks." *Newsweek*, 29 Mar. 2017, www.newsweek.com/london-attack-ira-terror-threat-severe-bomb-terrorism-573629.

15. McCann, Eamonn. "Real IRA's lust for violence matters more than ideology on the streets | Eamonn McCann." *The Guardian*, Guardian News and Media, 21 Aug. 2010, www.theguardian.com/uk/2010/aug/22/northern-ireland-dissidents-peace-process.

16. McDermott, Rose. *Political Psychology in International Relations*. Ann Arbor: U of Michigan, 2004. Print. For reference: Chapter 5: Behavior (119-152).

17. McDonald, Henry. "UK agents 'did have role in IRA bomb atrocities'." *The Observer*, Guardian News and Media, 9 Sept. 2006, www.theguardian.com/politics/2006/sep/10/uk.northernireland1.

18. Nietzsche, Friedrich Wilhelm. *Thus spake Zarathustra: a book for all and none*. Translated by Thomas Common, PDF ed., T. Common, 1908. For reference: Chapter IX: Preachers of Death (50-52), Chapter XXVI: THE PRIESTS (88-91), and Chapter XXXIV: Self-Surpassing (108-111).

19. Nietzsche, Friedrich Wilhelm. *THE ANTICHRIST*. Translated by H. L.

Mencken, The Project Gutenberg, 2006. For reference: Aphorisms 15, 16, 41, 43, 53, 54, and 55.

20. Nietzsche, Friedrich Wilhelm. *On the genealogy of morals: a polemical tract*. Translated by Ian Johnston, PDF, Richer Resources Publications, 2014.

21. POGATCHNIK, SHAWN. "IRA Proxy Bombings Kill 6 Troops, Civilian : Northern Ireland: The attack by the terrorist group is the deadliest against British forces in two years." *Los Angeles Times*, Los Angeles Times, 25 Oct. 1990, articles.latimes.com/1990-10-25/news/mn-4248_1_northern-ireland.

22. Webb, David. "Fritz Heider & Marianne Simmel: An Experimental Study of Apparent Behavior." *Psychology*, www.all-about-psychology.com/fritz-heider.html.

Chapter 4

1. "A Mathematical Proof That The Universe Could Have Formed Spontaneously From Nothing." *Medium*, The Physics ArXiv Blog, 11 Apr. 2014, medium.com/the-physics-arxiv-blog/a-mathematical-proof-that-the-universe-could-have-formed-spontaneously-from-nothing-ed7ed0f304a3.

2. Abels, Richard. "Crusades and early Christian attitudes toward warfare." *Academia.edu - Share research*, www.academia.edu/22844402/Crusades_and_early_Christian_attitudes_to ward_warfare. For reference: the original website for this has been removed from the US Naval Academy website when I first found it. Abels, Richard. "Timeline for the Crusades and Christian Holy War." Timeline for the Crusades and Christian Holy War. 2009. Web. 2016. <http://www.usna.edu/Users/history/abels/hh315/crusades_timeline.htm>

3. Baird, Julia. "Doubt as a Sign of Faith." *The New York Times*, The New York Times, 25 Sept. 2014, www.nytimes.com/2014/09/26/opinion/julia-baird-doubt-as-a-sign-of-faith.html.

4. "Christopher Hitchens Debates Al Sharpton - New York Public." *YouTube*, YouTube, 6 Dec. 2011, www.youtube.com/watch?v=HPYxA8dYLBY.

5. Cialdini, Robert B. *Influence: Science and practice*. 4th ed., 21st Century Bks, 2002. Chapter 1: Weapons of Influence (1-16), Chapter 2: Reciprocation (19-50), Chapter 3: Commitment and Consistency (52-95), Chapter 4: Social Proof (98-140), Chapter 6: Authority (178-200)

6. "Circular Reasoning." *Https://Www.logicallyfallacious.com*, www.logicallyfallacious.com/tools/lp/Bo/LogicalFallacies/66/Circular-Reasoning.

7. "Full text: bin Laden's 'letter to America'." *The Guardian*, Guardian News and Media, 24 Nov. 2002, www.theguardian.com/world/2002/nov/24/theobserver.

8. Gause, F. Gregory . "Getting It Backward on Iraq." *Foreign Affairs*, Foreign Affairs, 28 Jan. 2009, www.foreignaffairs.com/articles/iraq/1999-05-01/getting-it-backward-iraq.

9. Hedges, Chris. *War Is a Force That Gives Us Meaning*. PublicAffairs, 2002.

10. Ispas, Alexa. *Psychology and politics: a social identity perspective*. Psychology Press, 2014. For reference purposes, Chapter 1: Psychology and the Social Identity Perspective (1-24), Chapter 2: The Psychology of Social Influence (26-50)

11. Kahneman, Daniel. *Thinking, fast and slow*. Farrar, Straus and Giroux, 2015. For reference purposes: The Introduction (1-17), Chapter 4: The Associative Machine (50-58), Chapter 5: Cognitive Ease (59-70), Chapter 6:"Norms, Surprises, and Causes" (71-78), Chapter 7: A Machine for Jumping to Conclusions (79-88), Chapter 9: Answering an Easier Question (97-104), and Chapter 27: The Prospect Theory (278-288).

12. Lane, Christopher. "Losing Our Religion: Why Doubt Is a Passionate Exercise." *Psychology Today*, Sussex Publishers, 20 May 2011, www.psychologytoday.com/blog/side-effects/201105/losing-our-religion-why-doubt-is-passionate-exercise.

13. McDermott, Rose. *Political Psychology in International Relations*. Ann Arbor: U of Michigan, 2004. Print. For reference: Chapter 4: Cognition and Attitudes (77-117). Chapter 5: Behavior (119-152)

14. Mill, John Stuart. *Three essays on religion*. Timeless Wisdom Collection, 2016. For reference: c. Argument For a First Cause (71-77)

15. "Moving the Goalposts." *Https://Www.logicallyfallacious.com*, www.logicallyfallacious.com/tools/lp/Bo/LogicalFallacies/129/Moving-the-Goalposts.

16. Nietzsche, Friedrich Wilhelm. *The gay science (the joyful wisdom)*. Edited by Oscar Levy. Translated by Thomas Common, #52881, Gutenberg, 2016, www.gutenberg.org/files/52881/52881-h/52881-h.htm. For reference: Aphorism 341. The Heaviest Burden.—What if a demon crept after thee into thy loneliest loneliness some day or night, and said to thee: "This life, as thou livest it at present, and hast lived it, thou must live it once more, and also innumerable times; and there will be nothing new in it, but every pain and every joy and every thought and every sigh, and all the unspeakably small and great in thy life must come to thee again, and all in the same series and sequence—and similarly this spider and this moonlight among the trees, and similarly this moment, and I myself. The eternal sand-glass of existence will ever be turned once more, and thou with it, thou speck of dust!"—Wouldst thou not throw thyself down and gnash thy teeth, and curse the demon that so spake? Or hast thou once experienced a tremendous moment in which thou wouldst answer him: "Thou art a God, and never did I hear aught more divine!" If that thought acquired power

over thee, as thou art, it would transform thee, and perhaps crush thee; the question with regard to all and everything: "Dost thou want this once more, and also for innumerable times?" would lie as the heaviest burden upon thy activity! Or, how wouldst thou have to become favourably inclined to thyself and to life, so as to long for nothing more ardently than for this last eternal sanctioning and sealing?—

17. "No True Scotsman." *Https://Www.logicallyfallacious.com*, www.logicallyfallacious.com/tools/lp/Bo/LogicalFallacies/135/No-True-Scotsman.

18. "U.S. Religious Knowledge Survey." *Pew Research Center's Religion & Public Life Project*, Pew Research Center's Religion & Public Life Project, 19 Dec. 2017, www.pewforum.org/2010/09/28/u-s-religious-knowledge-survey/.

Chapter 5

1. "About Us." *Doctors Opposing Circumcision*, www.doctorsopposingcircumcision.org/about-us/#_statement-principles.

2. "Appeal to Tradition." *Https://Www.logicallyfallacious.com*, www.logicallyfallacious.com/tools/lp/Bo/LogicalFallacies/44/Appeal-to-Tradition.

3. Batrinos, Menelaos L. "Testosterone and Aggressive Behavior in Man." *International Journal of Endocrinology and Metabolism*, NCBI, 2012, www.ncbi.nlm.nih.gov/pmc/articles/PMC3693622/.

4. BEINER, THERESA M. "SEXY DRESSING REVISITED: DOES TARGET DRESS PLAY A PART IN SEXUAL HARASSMENT CASES? ." *Duke University School of Law*, Duke Journal of Gender Law & Policy, 2007, scholarship.law.duke.edu/cgi/viewcontent.cgi?&article=1109&context=djglp.   III. SOCIAL SCIENCE AND DRESS (143-148), IV. IMPLICATIONS OF DRESS FOR SEXUAL HARASSMENT LAW (148-151).

5. "BibleGateway." *Numbers 31:7-18 KJV - - Bible Gateway*, www.biblegateway.com/passage/?search=Numbers 31:7-18&version=KJV.

6. Boyle, G. J. "Issues associated with the introduction of circumcision into a non-Circumcising society." *Issues associated with the introduction of circumcision into a non-Circumcising society*, THE CIRCUMCISION REFERENCE LIBRARY, Nov. 2003, www.cirp.org/library/disease/HIV/boyle-sti/.

7. Bronselaer, G A, et al. "Male circumcision decreases penile sensitivity as measured in a large cohort." *BJU international.*, U.S. National Library of Medicine, May 2013, www.ncbi.nlm.nih.gov/pubmed/23374102.

8. Cialdini, Robert B. *Influence: Science and practice*. 4th ed., 21st Century Bks, 2002. Chapter 1: Weapons of Influence (1-16), Chapter 2: Reciprocation (19-50), Chapter 3: Commitment and Consistency (52-95), Chapter 4: Social Proof (98-140), Chapter 6: Authority (178-200).
9. Dweck, Carol S. *Mindset: How You Can Fulfill Your Potential*. Random House, 2012.
10. Freeman, Daniel, and Jason Freeman. "Why are men more likely than women to take their own lives?" *The Guardian*, Guardian News and Media, 21 Jan. 2015, www.theguardian.com/science/2015/jan/21/suicide-gender-men-women-mental-health-nick-clegg.
11. Freeman, David. "Circumcision Linked To Autism In Controversial New Study." *The Huffington Post*, TheHuffingtonPost.com, 20 Jan. 2015, www.huffingtonpost.com/2015/01/20/circumcision-autism-new-study_n_6503106.html.
12. Frisch, M, et al. "Male circumcision and sexual function in men and women: a survey-Based, cross-Sectional study in Denmark." *International journal of epidemiology.*, U.S. National Library of Medicine, Oct. 2011, www.ncbi.nlm.nih.gov/pubmed/21672947.
13. Frisch, Morten, and Jacob Simonsen. "Ritual circumcision and risk of autism spectrum disorder in 0- to 9-Year-Old boys: national cohort study in Denmark." *Journal of the Royal Society of Medicine*, SAGE Publications, July 2015, www.ncbi.nlm.nih.gov/pmc/articles/PMC4530408/.
14. Frisch, Morten, and Jacob Simonsen. "Ritual circumcision and risk of autism spectrum disorder in 0- to 9-Year-Old boys: national cohort study in Denmark." *Journal of the Royal Society of Medicine*, vol. 108, no. 7, Aug. 2015, pp. 266–279., doi:10.1177/0141076814565942.
15. Goldman, R. "The psychological impact of circumcision." *Circumcision Resource Center*, THE CIRCUMCISION REFERENCE LIBRARY, www.cirp.org/library/psych/goldman1/.
16. Green, Laci. "I LOVE FORESKIN (Wtf circumcision?)." *YouTube*, YouTube, 14 Aug. 2013, www.youtube.com/watch?v=JbTdkWV89Ak.
17. Green, Laci. "WHY I'M A...FEMINIST *Gasp*." *YouTube*, YouTube, 23 Apr. 2014, www.youtube.com/watch?v=UwJRFClybmk.
18. Green, Laci. "THE F-WORD." *YouTube*, YouTube, 8 July 2014, www.youtube.com/watch?v=EJPT_U97lNs.
19. Green, Laci. "TOXIC MASCULINITY!" *YouTube*, YouTube, 20 Dec. 2017, www.youtube.com/watch?v=i5juyXjDnJ0.
20. Grinnell, Renée. "Just-World Hypothesis." *Encyclopedia of Psychology*, 17 July 2016, psychcentral.com/encyclopedia/just-world-hypothesis/.
21. Healy, Melissa. "In addition to fueling aggression, testosterone can also make men more generous, study says." *Los Angeles Times*, Los Angeles Times, 26 Sept. 2016, www.latimes.com/science/sciencenow/la-sci-sn-

testosterone-behavior-men-20160926-snap-story.html.

22. "Infant Responses to Circumcision." *Circumcision Resource Center*, circumcision.org/infant-responses-to-circumcision/.

23. Kahneman, Daniel. *Thinking, fast and slow*. Farrar, Straus and Giroux, 2015. For reference purposes: Chapter 6:"Norms, Surprises, and Causes" (71-78), Chapter 8: How Judgments Happen (89-96), and Chapter 9: Answering an Easier Question (97-104).

24. Konner, Melvin. "MUTILATED IN THE NAME OF TRADITION." *The New York Times*, The New York Times, 14 Apr. 1990, www.nytimes.com/1990/04/15/books/mutilated-in-the-name-of-tradition.html. For reference: "Between 90 million and 100 million women of all ages now living in Africa had their childhoods interrupted by a traditional operation in which the clitoris is partly or, more commonly, completely removed - without anesthesia, with crude cutting tools and with little or no precaution against infection. In most cases clitoral excision is followed by another operation, in which the labia are partly cut away and then sewn together. Once a girl has healed, her vagina is almost completely sealed, leaving her a "pinhole" opening, only large enough for urine to pass drop by drop.The immediate consequences of this operation sometimes include hemorrhage, tetanus and other infections, excruciating pain and death. More common results include painful urination, backup of menstrual blood and severe pain during sexual intercourse. (Two to 12 weeks are required for gradual penetration, which is essentially a process of repeated tearing; for convenience, the honeymoon hotel in the Sudanese city of Port Sudan is next to a hospital.) Traditionally women are resewn after the birth of each child ("renewable virginity") only to experience the same effects again."

25. Kovac, Sarah. "New autism dispute: is circumcision a factor?" *Time*, Time, time.com/4314388/new-autism-dispute-is-circumcision-a-factor/.

26. Lightfoot-Klein, Hanny . *National Organization of Circumcision Resource Centers*, NOCIRC, Mar. 1994, www.nocirc.org/symposia/third/hanny3.html. For reference: Contrary to all my expectations, I discovered that this ancient custom as adhered to and defended most resolutely not by men, but by its survivors, the women elders. It was these women that insisted most vehemently on its perpetuation and it was they who also wielded the knife. Among the elite, the mutilation was often plotted by "the grandmothers," and carried out at the first unguarded moment that presented itself, in spite of all efforts that the child's educated parents had exerted in order to prevent it. To nearly all the population, male and female alike, the mere idea that a girl should not be "circumcised" was altogether unthinkable. Not only would such a girl find no one who would marry her, but it was generally believed that all sorts of evils in respect to her sexual behavior, her health,

and even more importantly in these cultures, the health of her husband and babies, would inevitably follow.   Eighty-seven percent of men and 83 percent of women voiced their unqualified approval of the practice, according to Dareer's extensive statistical study in Sudan. Taking into consideration that these mutilations are illegal under current Sudanese law, it is almost inevitable that the true approval rate is far closer to 100 percent for both men and women.   I learned that only a tiny handful of the most highly educated Africans had any notion whatsoever that in most of the world "female circumcision" was not practiced at all. Certainly, in the part of sub-Saharan East Africa where I researched the topic most intensively, a vulva left in its natural state stigmatized the woman as a slave, a prostitute, an outcast, an unclean being unworthy of the honor of continuing a respected family lineage.   Among the many people in all walks of life that I interviewed on the subject of female genital mutilation in Sudan, the epicenter of the most extreme excisions and infibulations, there was a young veterinarian who related the following to me:"It had simply never occurred to me that there was anything wrong with the practice. Nor had this apparently ever occurred to any of my contemporaries, with whom I had at one time or another discussed it. It was only when I studied at a European university and saw how much less complicated things were for women there, that I finally understood how terrible a thing it is."

27. Mims, Christopher. "Strange but True: Testosterone Alone Does Not Cause Violence." *Scientific American*, 5 July 2007, www.scientificamerican.com/article/strange-but-true-testosterone-alone-doesnt-cause-violence/.

28. Myers, A, and J Myers. *Rolling out male circumcision as a mass HIV/AIDS intervention seems neither justified nor practicable*, www.cirp.org/library/disease/HIV/myers2008/.

29. Myers, J. "Male circumcision and HIV infection." *History of Circumcision*, Historyofcircumcision.net, www.historyofcircumcision.net/index.php?option=content&task=view&id=85.

30. Narvaez, Darcia. "More Circumcision Myths You May Believe: Hygiene and STDs." *Psychology Today*, Sussex Publishers, 13 Sept. 2011, www.psychologytoday.com/blog/moral-landscapes/201109/more-circumcision-myths-you-may-believe-hygiene-and-stds.

31. Narvaez, Darcia. "Myths about Circumcision You Likely Believe." *Psychology Today*, Sussex Publishers, 11 Sept. 2011, www.psychologytoday.com/blog/moral-landscapes/201109/myths-about-circumcision-you-likely-believe.

32. Narvaez, Darcia. "Circumcision's Psychological Damage." *Psychology Today*, Sussex Publishers, 11 Jan. 2015, www.psychologytoday.com/blog/moral-landscapes/201501/circumcision-

s-psychological-damage.
33. Nietzsche, Friedrich Wilhelm. *On the genealogy of morals: a polemical tract*. Translated by Ian Johnston, PDF, Richer Resources Publications, 2014.
34. Page, Gayle Giboney. "Are There Long-Term Consequences of Pain in Newborn or Very Young Infants?" *The Journal of Perinatal Education*, U.S. National Library of Medicine, 2004, www.ncbi.nlm.nih.gov/pmc/articles/PMC1595204/.
35. Storr, Will. "The rape of men: the darkest secret of war." *The Observer*, Guardian News and Media, 16 July 2011, www.theguardian.com/society/2011/jul/17/the-rape-of-men.
36. "Till death do us part: A Post and Courier Special Report." *Post and Courier*, 19 Aug. 2014, www.postandcourier.com/app/till-death/partone.html.

Author's Influences:

Demonstrable scientific evidence, JK Rowling, Alexa Ispas, Beau Lotto, Daniel Gilbert, Robert Cialdini, Laci Green, Vlogbrothers Hank and John Green, Ex-Muslims of North America, Mike Davis, Chris Hedges, Sam Harris, Christopher Hitchens, Julia Galef, Daniel Kahneman and Amos Tversky, Heidi Grant Halvorson, Melinda and Bill Gates and the Gates Foundation's selfless work and Gatesnotes, Hans Rosling, Glenn Greenwald and the Intercept, Shin Megami Tensei, Tales of the Abyss, Tales of Berseria, Erich Fromm, Amnesty International, Rollo May, Brihadaranyaka Upanishads (Except the disgusting Chapter 6), Chandogya Upanishads, Samkhya Philosophical thought, Bhagavad Gita chapters on selflessness and acceptance of all, and Friedrich Nietzsche.

About the Author

Jarin Jove is the pseudonym of Niraj Choudhary in his ill-conceived attempt at being clever by making a nickname based upon switching his first name and using the shortest name of his favorite planet in the solar system. He holds a Bachelors of Science in Political Science from the New York Institute of Technology (2012) and a Masters of Arts in Political Science from Long Island University (2016). His intersecting interests of understanding the psychology of politics, the influence of New Atheism in criticizing the human rights abuses of religion, his avid love of reading psychology books and Friedrich Nietzsche's main works, and especially, Julia Galef's activism in support of a more rational world is what inspired him to write this book in the hopes of making a small contribution to a much greater and global conversation. He is an ardent capitalist, but doesn't believe capitalism can fill the void of government services or social safety nets and is concerned about governments maintaining any legitimacy if such programs are entirely eroded.

He has a personal blog: **www.jarinjove.com**. He can be reached via email at **jovejarin@hotmail.com** and on Twitter via the handle **@NocturneDream**.

He uses another pseudonym, Jason D. Visaria, to write fantasy novels and is the author of a dark humor book called *Ku Cuck Klan: The Family Values* written in order to exercise his Free Speech rights to mock Neo-Nazis and White Nationalists.